AN ADAPTED CLASSIC

Hamlet

William Shakespeare

GLOBE FEARON
EDUCATIONAL PUBLISHER

A Division of Simon & Schuster
Upper Saddle River, New Jersey

Adapter: Emily Hutchinson
Project Editor: Kristen Shepos-Salvatore
Editorial Supervisor: Cary Pepper
Editorial Assistant: Kathleen Kennedy
Production Editor: Alan Dalgleish
Marketing Manager: Sandra Hutchison
Art Supervision: Patricia Smythe
Electronic Page Production: Luc Van Meerbeek
Illustrator and Cover Illustration: Thomas Sperling

Printed in the United States of America.
1 2 3 4 5 6 7 8 9 10   99 98 97 96

ISBN 0-835-91864-5

GLOBE FEARON EDUCATIONAL PUBLISHER
A Division of Simon & Schuster
Upper Saddle River, New Jersey

CONTENTS

ABOUT THE AUTHOR

There are many things we do not know for certain about William Shakespeare. It is believed he was born on April 26, 1564. He grew up in Stratford upon Avon, a small town in England. He married Anne Hathaway in 1582, when he was 18. They had three children, two girls and one boy. Shakespeare went to London, where he became successful as an actor, a playwright, and a poet. He belonged to a group of actors called The King's Men, who performed his plays. In 1599, The King's Men built a theater, which they named the Globe. The Globe became one of the best-known theaters in London. Shakespeare's plays were also performed at court, for Queen Elizabeth I and King James I. Shakespeare retired from the theater around 1613. He returned to Stratford, where he bought a house and land. William Shakespeare died on April 23, 1616. He is buried in Stratford.

Who really wrote Shakespeare's plays is one of literature's great mysteries. Some people say that one man could not have written so many excellent plays. Some people think that if one man did write them, it was not Shakespeare, because they believe he was poorly educated. Other people say he did write the plays that bear his name, and consider William Shakespeare the world's greatest playwright.

hardly any stage props. Sets were very simple. In fact, people in the audience needed great imaginations. For them, the same set might have to work as a street scene or a ballroom scene.

The rear of the stage had a small curtained area. This could be used as an inner room, a tomb, or a prison. There were balconies on the sides of the stage. These were used for upper decks of ships, balconies of houses, and prison windows.

When theaters were not available, plays were performed in public places, such as inns and taverns. This is one reason Elizabethan plays had so many speeches that could be delivered in loud voices. The playwright had to make sure the audience could hear everything.

These are just some of the physical differences between Elizabethan theater and today's theater. There is also another important difference. Women were not allowed to act. All parts were played by men. Most women's roles were played by boys. They were often recruited from the boys' choirs in London churches.

CAST OF CHARACTERS

HAMLET, PRINCE OF DENMARK
The only child of the dead King Hamlet, and nephew of the present ruler of Denmark

CLAUDIUS, KING OF DENMARK
Hamlet's uncle

GERTRUDE
Queen of Denmark and Hamlet's mother

GHOST
The ghost of Hamlet's murdered father

POLONIUS
The Lord Chamberlain and chief adviser to Claudius

HORATIO
A commoner and loyal friend of Hamlet

LAERTES
The son of Polonius and the brother of Ophelia

OPHELIA
The daughter of Polonius and the sister of Laertes

ROSENCRANTZ and **GUILDENSTERN**
Former schoolmates and friends of Hamlet

FORTINBRAS
Prince of Norway

VOLTIMAND and **CORNELIUS**
Danish courtiers

MARCELLUS, BERNARDO, and **FRANCISCO**
Guards at the castle of Elsinore

REYNALDO
A servant of Polonius

GRAVEDIGGERS, LORDS, ATTENDANTS and **SERVANTS**

Act 1

Scene 1

Elsinore. A platform before the castle. FRANCISCO *is standing at his post.* BERNARDO *enters.*

BERNARDO: Who's there?

FRANCISCO: You tell me! Identify yourself.

BERNARDO: Long live the king![1]

FRANCISCO: Bernardo?

BERNARDO: Yes. It is midnight, time for my watch.
    You can go to bed now, Francisco.

FRANCISCO: Thank you for relieving me.
    It is bitter cold, and I am sick at heart.

BERNARDO: Has it been quiet tonight?

FRANCISCO: Not a mouse stirring.

BERNARDO: Well, good night.
    If you meet Horatio and Marcellus,
    My partners on watch, tell them to hurry.

(HORATIO *and* MARCELLUS *enter.*)

FRANCISCO: I think I hear them. Halt!
    Who is there?

HORATIO: Friends to this castle.
    And loyal followers of the King.

FRANCISCO: Bernardo is waiting for you.
    My watch is over. So, good night to you.

(FRANCISCO *exits.*)

---

1. Long live the king! a password

MARCELLUS: Hello! Bernardo!

BERNARDO: Welcome, Horatio. Welcome, good Marcellus.

HORATIO: Has the thing appeared again tonight?

BERNARDO: I have seen nothing.

MARCELLUS (*to* BERNARDO): Horatio says
That it is only our fantasy.
He does not believe that we have seen
The dreaded sight twice already.
So I have asked him to come along
With us to stand watch tonight.
That way, if the apparition² comes again,
He may confirm what we have seen and speak to it.

HORATIO: It will not appear.

BERNARDO: Sit down awhile,
And let us tell you the story all over again.

HORATIO: Well, let us sit down.
I'm willing to listen.

BERNARDO: Last night, at about one o'clock,
Marcellus and I—

(*The* GHOST *enters.*)

MARCELLUS: Quiet! Look over there!
It comes again!

BERNARDO: It looks just like the dead King.

MARCELLUS: You are a scholar, Horatio. Speak to it.

BERNARDO: Doesn't it look like the King, Horatio?

HORATIO: Yes. It fills me with fear and wonder.

BERNARDO: It wants to be spoken to.

---

2. apparition ghost

HORATIO: Who are you, who dares to wear the armor
  In which our dead King sometimes marched?
  In heaven's name, I order you, speak!

MARCELLUS: It is offended.

BERNARDO: See, it stalks away!

HORATIO: Stay! Speak, speak! I order you, speak!

(*The* GHOST *exits.*)

MARCELLUS: It is gone and will not answer.

BERNARDO: Now what do you think, Horatio?
  You tremble and look pale.
  Is this not something more than a fantasy?
  What do you think now?

HORATIO: Before my God, I did not believe it,
  But now I have seen it with my own eyes.

MARCELLUS: Is it not like the King?

HORATIO: As you are like yourself.
  That was the very armor the King wore
  When he met the King of Norway in battle.
  And he frowned just that way once, when angry.
  It is strange.

MARCELLUS: He has appeared like this twice before,
  And right at this time of night.

HORATIO: I have no idea what he wants,
  But, in my opinion, it is a bad omen.

MARCELLUS: Tell me, now, if you know,
  Why we have this nightly watch at the castle.
  And why do the ship-builders work day and night,
  With no time off even on Sunday?
  Why does our country seem to be preparing for war?

HORATIO: I have heard whispers about it. As you know,
Our last king, whose image just now appeared to us,
Was dared to fight by Norway's King Fortinbras.
When Fortinbras lost and was killed by our king,
He also lost the lands he had risked in the battle.
Now, sir, young Fortinbras, his son,
Has raised a force of men to recover the lands
Lost by his father. This, I take it, is the reason
For all the war preparation in our land.
It is troubling to my mind to remember
That before mighty Julius Caesar of Rome fell,
The graves stood empty, and the sheeted dead
Walked in the Roman streets.
Such apparitions are omens of fearful events.

(*The* GHOST *enters.*)

But quiet, look! It comes again!
Stay, illusion! If you have the use of voice,
Speak to me. (*The* GHOST *spreads its arms.*)
If I may do anything to help you, speak to me.
If you know anything about your country's fate,
Which, by knowing, we could avoid, speak!
Stay, and speak!

(*A rooster crows. The* GHOST *exits.*)

MARCELLUS: It is gone!

BERNARDO: It was about to speak,
When the rooster crowed.

HORATIO: And then it left, like a guilty thing
Following a fearful call. I have heard
That the rooster, the trumpet to the morning,
Awakes the god of day with his shrill sounds.
At his warning, any wandering spirit

Hurries to its grave. The truth of that story
Was just proven by the apparition's actions.
We must tell young Hamlet about this.
This spirit, silent to us, might speak to him.
Do you agree that we should tell him?

MARCELLUS: Let's do it. I know where to find him.

(ALL *exit.*)

Scene 2

A room of state in the castle. KING CLAUDIUS, QUEEN
GERTRUDE, VOLTIMAND, CORNELIUS, POLONIUS, LAERTES,
HAMLET, *and* LORDS *enter.*

KING: The memory of our[3] dear brother's death
    Is still fresh, our hearts are heavy with grief,
    And our whole kingdom has been full of woe.
    Yet, we must think of the good of the kingdom,
    Which must have leadership in this time of war.
    Therefore, we have taken as wife our former sister.[4]
    We have listened to your good advice, which has
    Freely gone along with this matter.
    For all, our thanks.
    Now you all know that young Fortinbras
    Supposes we are weak. He thinks that
    Our late brother's death has left our state
    In confusion and disorder.
    He hopes to take advantage of this,

---

3. our King Claudius is following the custom of royalty, referring to himself in the plural form.

4. our former sister Queen Gertrude is his former sister-in-
law; she had been married to his brother, the former King
Hamlet.

And he has pestered us with messages
About the surrender of those lands
Lost by his father to our most valiant brother.
But our brother won these lands legally.
We have written to the present King of Norway,
The uncle of young Fortinbras.
He is weak and bedridden, and he knows little
About his nephew's intentions. In this letter,
I ask him to order his nephew to leave us alone.
I ask you, good Cornelius, and you, Voltimand,
To bear this greeting to the King of Norway.
Farewell, and hurry back.

(KING CLAUDIUS *hands them a paper.* CORNELIUS *and*
VOLTIMAND *exit.*)

And now, Laertes, what's the news with you?
You spoke of a favor you wished. What is it?

LAERTES: My good lord, I ask your permission
And your blessing to return to France.
I came from there to Denmark willingly
To show my support for your coronation.
Now, I must confess, that duty done,
My thoughts and wishes bend again toward France.

KING: Do you have your father's permission?
What does Polonius say?

POLONIUS: My lord, he has received my permission
By his constant begging. At last, I agreed.
I do ask you, give him permission to go.

KING: Enjoy your youth, Laertes. Time is yours,
And you may spend it as you like.
And now, my nephew Hamlet, and my son—

HAMLET (*aside*[5]): I may be your nephew,
　　But I am hardly your son.

KING: Why do you still seem to be under a dark cloud?

HAMLET: Not so, my lord. I am too much in the sun.[6]

QUEEN: Good Hamlet, cast your gloomy spirit off,
　　And be a little friendlier to the King.
　　Stop mourning for your father.
　　You know all that lives must die,
　　Passing from nature to eternity.

HAMLET: Yes, madam, I know.

KING: It is sweet of you to mourn so much for your father.
　　But you must know, your father lost a father,
　　And that lost father also lost his.
　　The survivor is bound by obligation as a son
　　To mourn for a while. But to continue
　　To grieve for so long is stubborn and unmanly.
　　It is a fault against heaven, a fault against the dead,
　　And a fault against nature. Please stop grieving,
　　And think of us as your father.
　　You are heir to the throne, and I love you no less
　　Than I would love my own son. Your desire
　　To go back to school in Wittenberg[7]
　　Goes against everything we wish.
　　We ask you to stay here in Denmark,
　　Here in the cheer and comfort of our eye,

---

5. **aside**　a term used in plays to indicate that the speaker's words are meant just for the audience and cannot be heard by any of the other characters
6. **in the sun**　Hamlet is using sun to mean "in the favor of the court."
7. **Wittenberg**　German university founded in 1502

Our chief courtier,[8] cousin, and our son.

QUEEN: Answer your mother's prayers, Hamlet.
I ask you to stay with us; do not go to Wittenberg.

HAMLET: I shall do my best to obey you, madam.

KING: Why, it is a loving and a fair reply.

(*to* QUEEN GERTRUDE) Madam, come.

(ALL *exit but* HAMLET.)

HAMLET: Oh, that this too, too solid flesh
Would melt, thaw, and turn into dew!
Or that God had not said we must not commit suicide!
Oh, God! God!
How weary, stale, flat, and useless the world seems!
It is like an unweeded garden gone to seed.
That it should come to this!
Not even two months dead, so excellent a King!
He was so loving to my mother that he wouldn't
Even let the winds blow too roughly on her face.
Must I remember? Why, she would hang on him
As if her appetite grew by what it fed on.
And yet, within a month—let me not think of it!
Frailty, your name is woman!
Oh, God! A beast with no power to reason
Would have mourned longer!
Now, married to my uncle,
My father's brother, but no more like my father
Than I am like Hercules.[9] Within a month,
Before the salt of her tears had left her eyes,
She married. Oh, most wicked speed!

---

8. **courtier** a member of a ruler's court
9. **Hercules** a hero in Greek mythology famous for his great strength

This marriage will never come to any good.
But break, my heart, for I must hold my tongue.

(HORATIO, MARCELLUS, *and* BERNARDO *enter.*)

HORATIO: Hail to your lordship!

HAMLET: I am glad to see you well, Horatio!
And you, too, Marcellus and Bernardo.
What brings you here from Wittenberg?

HORATIO: My lord, I came to see your father's funeral.

HAMLET: Do not mock me, fellow student.
I think it was to see my mother's wedding.

HORATIO: Indeed, my lord, it followed soon after.

HAMLET: Thrift, thrift, Horatio! The funeral meats
Were served cold at the marriage tables.
I would rather have met my dearest foe in heaven,
Than to ever have seen that day, Horatio!
My father!—I think I see my father.

HORATIO (*surprised*): Where, my lord?

HAMLET: In my mind's eye, Horatio.

HORATIO: I saw him once. He was a good king.

HAMLET: He was a man, all in all.
I shall not look upon his like again.

HORATIO: My lord, I think I saw him last night.

HAMLET: Saw? Who?

HORATIO: My lord, the King your father.

HAMLET: The King my father!

HORATIO: Yes, and these two gentlemen did, too.
Marcellus and Bernardo saw him
Two nights in a row, while on watch,
After midnight. A figure like your father,

Dressed from head to foot in armor,
Appeared before them. They were so afraid
That they did not speak to him.
They told me about it, and I kept watch
With them on the third night.
It happened again, at the same time of night.
I knew your father. The Ghost looked just like him.

HAMLET: Did you not speak to it?

HORATIO: My lord, I did.
But it did not answer. It seemed ready to,
But just then the morning rooster crowed,
And at the sound, it hurried away,
And vanished from our sight.

HAMLET: It is very strange.

HORATIO: As I do live, my honored lord, it is true.
We thought it was our duty to let you know of it.

HAMLET: Indeed, indeed, sirs, but this troubles me.
Are you on watch tonight?

BERNARDO *and* MARCELLUS: We are, my lord.

HAMLET: He was dressed in armor, you say?

BERNARDO *and* MARCELLUS: Yes, my lord.

HAMLET: Then how did you see his face?

HORATIO: He wore his visor up.

HAMLET: Was he frowning?

HORATIO: He looked more sad than angry.

HAMLET: I wish I had been there.
I will watch with you tonight.
Perhaps it will walk again.
If it looks like my father, I will speak to it.
Tell no one about this. I'll see you tonight,

Between eleven and twelve.

ALL: Until then, farewell.

(ALL *exit but* HAMLET.)

HAMLET: My father's spirit—in armor! All is not well.
I wish the night were already come!
Till then, sit still, my soul. Foul deeds will rise
Over attempts to hide them from men's eyes.

(HAMLET *exits.*)

Scene 3

A room in POLONIUS'S *house.* LAERTES *and* OPHELIA, *his sister, enter.*

LAERTES: My bags are already on board.
Farewell, my sister. Please write often.
As for Hamlet, and his attentions to you,
Do not take them too seriously.
They are like violets in the spring,
Fast-blooming and sweet, but not long-lasting.

OPHELIA: No more than that?

LAERTES: No. Perhaps he loves you now,
But remember who he is.
Because of his position, his will is not his own.
He may not, as other people do, choose his own wife,
For his choice affects the good of the whole state.
If he says he loves you, be very careful.
If you lose your honor or your heart,
You might also lose your good name.
Fear it, Ophelia, fear it, my dear sister.

OPHELIA: I shall take your words to my heart.
But, my good brother, I hope you follow

Your own advice, too.

(POLONIUS *enters.*)

POLONIUS: Are you still here, Laertes? Aboard, aboard!
    The wind sits in the shoulder of your sail,
    And everyone on the ship is waiting for you.
    But listen first. I have some advice for you.
    Be friendly, but by no means too friendly.
    Keep the friends you have
    And tie them to your soul with hoops of steel,
    But do not give the hand of friendship too easily
    To every new person you meet.
    Give every man your ear, but few your voice.
    Listen to criticism, but do not judge others.
    Buy clothing as costly as you can afford,
    And be sure it is good, but not gaudy,
    For clothing tells a lot about a man.
    Neither a borrower nor a lender be,
    For a loan often loses both the money and the friend,
    And borrowing dulls the edge of thriftiness.
    This above all: to your own self be true,
    And it must follow, as the night follows the day,
    You cannot then be false to any man.
    Farewell. My blessings go with you!

LAERTES: I humbly take my leave, my lord.
    (*to* OPHELIA) Farewell, Ophelia, and remember well
    What I have said to you.

(LAERTES *exits.*)

POLONIUS: What did he say to you, Ophelia?

OPHELIA: Something about the Lord Hamlet.

POLONIUS: Indeed. I am glad he did.
    I have heard that you and Hamlet

Have been spending a lot of time alone lately.
If that is true, I must tell you that
You don't understand what people might be saying.
What is between you? Tell me the truth.

OPHELIA: My lord, he has let me know
That he has affection for me.

POLONIUS: Affection! Do you believe him?

OPHELIA: I do not know, my lord, what I should think.

POLONIUS: Well, then, I will teach you.
If you believe his words, you are not only foolish,
But you'll make me look like a fool.

OPHELIA: My lord, he has courted me honorably.
And he has supported his words
With almost all the holy vows of heaven.

POLONIUS: Such words are like traps to catch birds.
I know how young men are, my daughter.
You should not make yourself so available to him.
In plain terms, from now on,
I do not want you to spend any of your leisure time
With the Lord Hamlet. Do not even talk to him.
These are my final words. Do as I say.

OPHELIA: I shall obey, my lord.

(POLONIUS *and* OPHELIA *exit.*)

Scene 4

A platform before the castle. HAMLET, HORATIO, *and*
MARCELLUS *enter.*

HAMLET: It is so cold out here!
What time is it?

HORATIO: I think it is almost midnight.

MARCELLUS: No, it already struck midnight.

HORATIO: Indeed? I did not hear it. Then it is close
   To the time when the spirit takes its walk.

(*The* GHOST *enters.*)

   Look, my lord, it comes!

HAMLET: May the angels help us!
   Whether you come for good or for evil,
   You come in a form that is easy for me to speak to.
   I'll call you Hamlet, King, father, royal Dane.
   Oh, answer me! Tell me why your dead bones
   Have burst their burial clothes. Why has your tomb
   Opened its marble jaws and let you out again?
   What does this mean, that you, a dead corpse,
   Visit us, wearing a suit of armor? Why?
   What for? What should we do?

(*The* GHOST *beckons to* HAMLET.)

HORATIO: It beckons you to go away with it.

MARCELLUS: Do not go!

HORATIO: No, by no means.

HAMLET: It will not speak unless I follow it.

HORATIO: Do not go, my lord.

HAMLET: Why not? What should I fear?
   My life is not worth the price of a pin.
   As for my soul, what can it do to that?
   It waves me forth again. I'll follow it.

HORATIO: What if it leads you to danger
   Or into madness? Think about it.

HAMLET: It waves to me still.
   (*to the* GHOST) Go on. I'll follow you.

MARCELLUS (*holding him back*): Do not go, my lord.

HAMLET: Take your hands away!

HORATIO: Do as we say. You shall not go!

HAMLET: My fate cries out.
   Every vein in my body is as brave as a lion.
   Unhand me, gentlemen! I say, get away!
   (*to the* GHOST) Go on, I'll follow you.

(*The* GHOST *and* HAMLET *exit.*)

MARCELLUS: Let's follow him.

HORATIO: What for? What good will that do?

MARCELLUS: Something is rotten
   In the state of Denmark.

HORATIO: Heaven will take care of it.

MARCELLUS: No! Let's follow him.

(HORATIO *and* MARCELLUS *exit.*)

Scene 5

Another part of the platform. The GHOST *and* HAMLET
enter.

HAMLET: Where will you lead me? Speak.
   I will go no further.

GHOST: Listen to me. My hour is almost come,
   When I must give myself to the tormenting flames.

HAMLET: Alas, poor ghost!

GHOST: Do not pity me, but listen to my words.

HAMLET: Speak. I am bound to hear.

GHOST: And you will be bound to revenge,
   When you hear.

HAMLET: What?

GHOST: I am your father's spirit,
Doomed for a certain time to walk the night,
And for the day confined to the fires
Till the foul crimes done during my life
Are burned away. If I were not forbidden
To tell the secrets of my prison-house, I could tell
A tale that would freeze your young blood,
Make your eyes fall from their sockets,
And make your hair stand on end
Like the quills on a frightened porcupine.
But this eternal tale must not be told
To ears of flesh and blood. Listen, oh, listen!
If you ever did love your dear father—

HAMLET: Oh, God!

GHOST: Revenge his foul and most unnatural murder.

HAMLET: Murder!

GHOST: Murder most foul, as murder always is,
But this was the most foul, strange, and unnatural.

HAMLET: Tell me what happened, so I,
With wings as swift as thoughts of love,
May sweep to my revenge.

GHOST: Hamlet, listen to me:
The story is being told that, while I was sleeping
In my garden, a serpent stung me. All of Denmark
Believes that this is what happened. But know this,
Noble youth, the serpent that stung your father
Now wears his crown.

HAMLET: Oh, just as I thought! My uncle!

GHOST: Yes, that beast. First he stole my Queen.
Oh, Hamlet, what a fall that was for her!

To go from me, whose love was so true,
To that wretch who was so far below me.
But quickly: I think I can smell the morning air.
I will be brief. I was sleeping in my garden,
As was my custom in the afternoon,
When your uncle poured poison into my ears.
The poison he used was swift as quicksilver.
It coursed through my whole body
And killed me almost instantly.
Thus, while I was sleeping, I was killed
By my own brother's hand. In one moment,
I was deprived of life, of crown, and of queen.
Cut off before receiving the last sacraments,
With no chance to repent for my sins, but sent
To the next world with all my sins on my head.
Oh, horrible! Oh, horrible! Most horrible!
If you have any feelings in you, you must avenge me.
But whatever you do,
⁕ Do not harm your mother: leave her to heaven
And to those thorns that lie inside her heart,
To prick and sting her. Farewell at once!
It is almost dawn. Farewell! Remember me.

(*The* GHOST *exits.*)

HAMLET: Remember you! Yes, from my memory
    I'll wipe away all foolish records,
    All advice from books, all past impressions
    That youth put there.
    Your commandment alone shall live in my mind.
    Yes, by heaven! Oh, most evil woman!
    Oh, villain, villain, smiling, evil villain!
    One may smile, and smile, and be a villain.
    So, uncle, there you are. Now to my promise:

"Remember me." I have sworn it.

HORATIO (*from offstage*): My lord! My lord!

MARCELLUS (*from offstage*): Lord Hamlet!

(HORATIO *and* MARCELLUS *enter.*)

MARCELLUS: What happened, my noble lord?

HORATIO: What news, my lord?

HAMLET: Oh, wonderful!

HORATIO: My good lord, tell us.

HAMLET: No, you will reveal it.

HORATIO: Not I, my lord, by heaven!

HAMLET: Then you'll keep this a secret?

HORATIO *and* MARCELLUS: Yes, by heaven, my lord.

HAMLET: There's a villain living in Denmark.

HORATIO: We didn't need a ghost from the grave
    To tell us that, my lord.

HAMLET: Why, you are right.
    And now, good friends,
    As you are friends, scholars, and soldiers,
    Give me one poor request.

HORATIO: What is it, my lord?

HAMLET: Tell no one what you have seen tonight.

BOTH: My lord, we will not.

HAMLET: Swear it.

HORATIO: I will not say a thing, my lord.

MARCELLUS: Nor will I, my lord.

HAMLET: Swear it, upon my sword.

MARCELLUS: We have sworn, my lord, already.

HAMLET: Indeed, upon my sword, indeed.

GHOST (*from beneath the stage*): Swear!

HORATIO: State the oath, my lord.

HAMLET: Never to speak of this that you have seen.
Swear by my sword.

GHOST (*from beneath*): Swear.

HAMLET: Come here, gentlemen,
And lay your hands again upon my sword:
Swear by my sword
Never to speak of this that you have heard.

GHOST (*from beneath*): Swear by his sword.

HORATIO: Oh, this is strange!

HAMLET: And therefore as a stranger, welcome it.
There are more things in heaven and earth, Horatio,
Than are dreamt of in your philosophy.
But come—
Here, as before, swear once again.

GHOST (*from beneath*): Swear.

HAMLET: Rest, rest, troubled spirit!
(HORATIO *and* MARCELLUS *swear.*) So, gentlemen,
With all my love, I do thank you.
Let us go in together,
And, remember, not a word about this!
The time is out of joint. Oh, cursed spite,
That ever I was born to set it right!
Now, come. Let us go together.

(ALL *exit.*)

Act 2

Scene 1

A room in the house of POLONIUS. POLONIUS *and*
REYNALDO *enter.*

POLONIUS: Give Laertes this money and these notes.

REYNALDO: I will, my lord.

POLONIUS: I would appreciate it, good Reynaldo,
　　If you would ask some questions about his behavior
　　Before you go to visit him.

REYNALDO: My lord, I intended to do that.

POLONIUS: Well said, very well said. Find out first
　　Which Danes are in Paris. Find out were they go,
　　What they do, and who their friends are.
　　As you talk to people about these things,
　　Some of them might mention that they know my son.
　　Then you can pretend some slight knowledge of him.
　　You could say, "I know his father and his friends,
　　And I know him a little." Understand, Reynaldo?

REYNALDO: Yes, very well, my lord.

POLONIUS: You could say, "I know him a little,
　　But not very well. If I remember correctly,
　　He's very wild, addicted to such and such."
　　And then you could say whatever you please.
　　Mind you, don't say anything to dishonor him.
　　Be careful of that. But, sir, you could mention
　　Such reckless, wild, and usual slips
　　That are common to youth and liberty.

REYNALDO: Such as gambling, my lord?

POLONIUS: Yes, or drinking, fencing, swearing,
    Quarreling, things like that. Speak of his faults
    In such a way that they seem very minor,
    The flash and outbreak of a fiery mind,
    The wildness common to men his age.

REYNALDO: But, my good lord—

POLONIUS: Why should you do this?
    Well, sir, here's my purpose,
    And, I believe, this will work:
    As you speak of my son's slight faults,
    The person you speak to might say,
    "I know that gentleman.
    I saw him yesterday, or the other day,
    Or then, or then, with such and such.
    And, as you say, there was gambling."
    Or, maybe the person would say,
    "I saw him enter such and such
    A place where there was drinking,"
    Or so forth. Listen now,
    Your bait of falsehood might catch a fish of truth.
    And thus we will be able to find out
    What Laertes has been doing.
    You understand me, do you not?

REYNALDO: My lord, I do.

POLONIUS: Good-bye then. Fare you well.

REYNALDO: Farewell.

(REYNALDO *exits.* OPHELIA *enters.*)

POLONIUS: Ophelia! What's the matter?

OPHELIA: Oh, my lord, my lord,
    I have been so frightened.

POLONIUS: With what, in the name of God?

OPHELIA: My lord, as I was sewing in my room,
  Lord Hamlet, with his shirt all unbuttoned,
  No hat on his head, his stockings dirty
  And falling down on his ankle,
  Pale as his shirt, his knees knocking each other,
  And with a look I can barely describe—
  He came before me.

POLONIUS: Mad for your love?

OPHELIA: My lord, I do not know,
  But truly, I do fear it.

POLONIUS: What did he say?

OPHELIA: He took me by the wrist and held me hard,
  And held his other hand to his forehead.
  He started looking at my face so closely,
  As if he wanted to draw it. For a long time
  He stayed that way. At last, he shook my arm a little
  And waved his head up and down,
  And raised a sigh so terrible and deep
  That it seemed to shatter his body
  And end his being. That done, he let me go,
  And turning his head over his shoulder,
  He seemed to find his way without his eyes,
  For he went out of my room without their help,
  And to the last, kept looking back at me.

POLONIUS: Come, go with me. I will go seek the King.
  This is the very madness of love,
  Whose violent character destroys itself
  And leads a man to desperate deeds,
  As often as any passion under heaven
  That affects our natures. I am sorry—
  Have you given him any hard words lately?

OPHELIA: No, my good lord. But, as you commanded,
I refused his letters and denied him my company.

POLONIUS: That has made him mad.
I am sorry that I misunderstood him.
I thought he was just toying with you
And meant to ruin you. Perhaps I am just too jealous!
Come, we will go to the King.
This sort of thing, if kept secret, could lead
To far more grief than any of us need.

(OPHELIA *and* POLONIUS *exit.*)

Scene 2

A room in the castle. KING, QUEEN, ROSENCRANTZ,
GUILDENSTERN, *and* ATTENDANTS *enter.*

KING: Welcome, dear Rosencrantz and Guildenstern!
Thank you for coming on such short notice.
It's good to see you. I'm sure that you have heard
Of the changes in Hamlet. He seems different
Both inside and out. What might have caused this,
Other than his father's death, I cannot imagine.
I beg you both, since you have been friends of his
Since childhood, to rest here in our court
For a short time. By your company, perhaps you can
Draw him on to pleasures and also find out
As much as you can about what is bothering him.
Perhaps we could help him,
If we knew what was wrong.

QUEEN: Good gentlemen, he has talked of you often.
I am sure there are no two men living
To whom he feels closer than he does to you.
If it will please you to spend some time here,
Your visit shall be royally rewarded.

ROSENCRANTZ: Both your Majesties
  Might, by the power you have over us,
  Choose to command rather than ask.

GUILDENSTERN: But we both obey,
  And offer our services freely.

KING: Thanks, Rosencrantz and gentle Guildenstern.

QUEEN: Thanks, Guildenstern and gentle Rosencrantz.
  (to ATTENDANTS) Go, some of you,
  And bring these gentlemen to where Hamlet is.

GUILDENSTERN: May our presence and our practices
  Be pleasant and helpful to him!

(ROSENCRANTZ, GUILDENSTERN, *and some* ATTENDANTS *exit.* POLONIUS *enters.*)

POLONIUS: The ambassadors from Norway, my good lord,
  Have joyfully returned.

KING: You always have good news!

POLONIUS: Have I, my lord? I assure you, your Majesty,
  That I hold my duty as seriously as I hold my soul.
  And I do think that I have found
  The very cause of Hamlet's madness.

KING: Oh, speak of that. I long to hear it.

POLONIUS: First, listen to the ambassadors.
  My news shall be the dessert to that great feast.

KING: Very well. Bring them in.

(POLONIUS *exits. The* KING *speaks to the* QUEEN.)

  He tells me, my dear Gertrude, that he has found
  The reason and cause of your son's
  Strange behavior.

QUEEN: I doubt that it is anything but the main point,

His father's death and our quick marriage.

(POLONIUS *enters with* VOLTIMAND *and* CORNELIUS.)

Welcome, my good friends!
What news do you have from Norway?

VOLTIMAND: The King of Norway sends his greetings.
When he received your letter, he sent out orders
To his nephew to stop preparing for war with you.
He had thought that his nephew
Was preparing to fight Poland. When he discovered
That the preparations were against your Highness,
He ordered young Fortinbras to stop.
In brief, Fortinbras obeys his uncle.
The King of Norway, overjoyed, gave his nephew
Enough money to take his soldiers against Poland.

(VOLTIMAND *gives the* KING *a paper.*)

The King of Norway asks your permission,
As written in this document,
For his nephew to march through Denmark
On the way to Poland.

KING: This pleases us. When we have more time,
We'll read, answer, and think about this business.
Meanwhile, we thank you for your efforts.
Go to your rest. Tonight, we'll feast together.
Welcome home!

(VOLTIMAND *and* CORNELIUS *exit.*)

POLONIUS: That was good news.
Now, since brevity[1] is the soul of wit,
I will be brief. Your noble son is mad.

---

1. **brevity** briefness; shortness

Mad I call it, for, to define true madness,
What is it but to be nothing else but mad?
But let that go.

QUEEN: Get to the point.

POLONIUS: That he is mad, it is true.
It is true that it is a pity.
And it is a pity that it is true.
But, to the point:
Let us say that he is mad. Now it remains
That we find out the cause of this effect,
Or rather, the cause of this defect.
I have a daughter—I have her while she is mine—
Who, in her duty and obedience,
Has given me this letter. Listen:

(POLONIUS *reads from a letter.*)

"To the heavenly and my soul's idol, the most
    beautified Ophelia—"
What a stupid word, a vile word; "beautified" is a vile
    word. But you shall hear more. Listen:
"Doubt that the stars are fire,
Doubt that the sun does move,
Doubt truth to be a liar,
But never doubt I love.
Oh, dear Ophelia, I am no good at poetry. But I love
you so much. Oh, please believe me. Farewell.
Yours forever, most dear lady,
As long as I live,
Hamlet."
In obedience, my daughter has shown me this letter.
And more than this, she tells me what he says to her.

KING: But how has she received his love?

POLONIUS: What do you think of me?

KING: As a faithful and honorable man.

POLONIUS: I hope that I always prove so.
But what might you think,
If I had done nothing when I heard about this love?
No, I went straight to my daughter and said,
"Lord Hamlet is a prince out of your reach.
This must not be." And then I told her
That she should stay away from him,
Admit no messengers, receive no gifts.
She took my advice, and he, rejected,
Fell into a sadness, then into a fast,
Then into sleeplessness, then into weakness,
Then into the madness in which he now raves,
And that we all mourn for.

KING: Do you think this is the reason?

QUEEN: It may be; it makes sense.

POLONIUS: Has there ever been a time
That I have positively said, "It is so,"
When it proved otherwise?

KING: Not that I know.

POLONIUS: Then believe me now.

(*He points to his head and shoulders.*)

Take this from this, if I'm not right.
And if you'll let me, I'll prove it.

KING: How may we test your idea?

POLONIUS: You know that sometimes he walks for hours
At a time, here in the lobby.
At such a time, I'll make sure that
Ophelia is nearby.

You and I can hide behind the wall tapestry then.
We'll watch their meeting. If he does not love her,
And hasn't lost his mind because of it,
Then I will stop being an assistant for a king,
But keep a farm instead.

KING: We will try it.

(HAMLET *enters, reading a book.*)

QUEEN: See how sadly the poor wretch comes, reading.

POLONIUS: Go away, I do beg you both.
I'll speak to him immediately. Please leave.

(KING, QUEEN, *and* ATTENDANTS *exit.*)

How are you, my good Lord Hamlet?

HAMLET: Well, thank you. And you?

POLONIUS: Do you know me, my lord?

HAMLET: Very well. You sell fish.

POLONIUS: Not I, my lord.

HAMLET: Then I wish you were so honest a man.

POLONIUS: Honest, my lord?

HAMLET: Yes, sir. To be honest, as this world goes, is to be one man out of ten thousand.

POLONIUS: That's very true, my lord.

HAMLET: Do you have a daughter?

POLONIUS: I have, my lord.

HAMLET: Do not let her walk in the sun. Conception[2]

---

2. conception Hamlet is playing on two meanings of the word. One meaning is "understanding." Another meaning is "becoming pregnant."

is a blessing, but as your daughter may conceive[3]—Friend, look to it.

POLONIUS (*aside*): Listen to him. Still talking about my daughter, yet he knew me not at first, and said I sold fish. He is far gone. Truly, in my own youth, I suffered much for love—almost as much as this. I'll speak to him again. (*to* HAMLET) What do you read, my lord?

HAMLET: Words, words, words.

POLONIUS: What is the matter, my lord?

HAMLET: Between who?

POLONIUS: I mean, the matter that you read, my lord.

HAMLET: Lies, sir. This writer says here that old men have gray beards, that their faces are wrinkled, that their eyes are runny, that they lack brains and have weak legs. All of this, sir, I do strongly believe, yet I say it is not honest to have it written down like this.

POLONIUS (*aside*): Though this be madness, yet there is method in it. (*to* HAMLET) Will you walk out of the air, my lord?

HAMLET: Into my grave?

POLONIUS: Indeed, that is out of the air. (*aside*) How wise his replies sometimes are! I will leave him, and figure out a way of getting him and my daughter to meet. (*to* HAMLET) My lord, I will take my leave of you.

HAMLET: You cannot, sir, take from me anything that I will not give up more willingly—except my life, except my life, except my life.

---

3. conceive Again, Hamlet is playing on two meanings. One meaning is "to understand." Another meaning is "to become pregnant."

POLONIUS: Farewell, my lord.

(POLONIUS *exits.*)

HAMLET (*aside*): These tiresome old fools!

(ROSENCRANTZ *and* GUILDENSTERN *enter.*)

GUILDENSTERN (*to* HAMLET): My honored lord!

ROSENCRANTZ: My most dear lord!

HAMLET: My excellent good friends! How are you, Guildenstern? Ah, Rosencrantz! How are you both?

ROSENCRANTZ: As the ordinary children of the earth.

GUILDENSTERN: Happy that we are not unhappy. On Fortune's cap, we are not the very button.[4]

HAMLET: Nor the soles of her shoe?

ROSENCRANTZ: Neither, my lord.

HAMLET: Then you live about her waist, Or in the middle of her favors?

GUILDENSTERN: Exactly so, my lord.

HAMLET: What news do you have?

ROSENCRANTZ: None, my lord, but that the world's grown honest.

HAMLET: Then the end of the world must be near. But your news is not true. Let me ask you this, my good friends: what have you done to Fortune, that caused her to send you to this prison?

GUILDENSTERN: Prison, my lord?

HAMLET: Denmark's a prison.

ROSENCRANTZ: Then the world is one.

---

4. button the highest point on a hat

HAMLET: A big one, in which there are many rooms and dungeons. Denmark is one of the worst.

ROSENCRANTZ: We do not think so, my lord.

HAMLET: Why, then, it is not a prison to you, for nothing is either good or bad unless you think it is. To me, Denmark is a prison.

ROSENCRANTZ: Why, then, your ambition makes it one. It is too narrow for your mind.

HAMLET: Oh, God, I could be inside a nutshell and count myself a king of infinite space, except for the fact that I have bad dreams.

GUILDENSTERN: Those dreams are ambition, for ambition is merely the shadow of a dream.

HAMLET: A dream itself is but a shadow.

ROSENCRANTZ: Truly. And I believe that ambition is so airy and light that it is but a shadow's shadow.

HAMLET: Shall we go to the court? For, I tell you, I cannot think about this any longer.

BOTH: We'll wait upon you.

HAMLET: No, you won't. I will not put you with the rest of my servants, for to speak to you like an honest man, I am most dreadfully waited upon. But in the familiar course of friendship, what brings you here to Elsinore?

ROSENCRANTZ: To visit you, my lord; no other reason.

HAMLET: Beggar that I am, I am even poor in thanks. But I thank you. Were you not asked to come? Was it your own idea? Is it a free visit? Come, come, tell me the truth. Come, come. Speak to me.

GUILDENSTERN: What should we say, my lord?

HAMLET: Why, anything, but tell the truth. You were sent for. I can tell by the way you are acting. I know the good king and queen have sent for you.

ROSENCRANTZ: Why would they do that, my lord?

HAMLET: That, you must tell me. In the name of our friendship, I ask you to tell me the truth.

ROSENCRANTZ (*aside to* GUILDENSTERN): What do you say?

GUILDENSTERN (*to* HAMLET): My lord, we were sent for.

HAMLET: I will tell you why. That way, you won't have to break your word to the King and Queen. Lately, I have—I don't know why—lost all my happiness, stopped exercising. Indeed, I feel so bad that the whole earth seems nothing more than a dead rock. And the air, this majestic roof topped with golden fire, why, it seems to me nothing more than a foul and poisonous collection of gases. What a piece of work is a man! How noble in reason! How boundless in mind! In form and motion, how graceful and admirable! In action, how like an angel! In understanding, how like a god! The beauty of the world! The highest of animals! And yet, to me, what is this piece of dust? Man does not delight me; nor does woman, though by your smiling you seem to say so.

ROSENCRANTZ: My lord, I had no such thoughts.

HAMLET: Why did you laugh, then, when I said "Man does not delight me"?

ROSENCRANTZ: I was thinking, my lord, if man does not delight you, the actors who are coming will get a dull welcome. We met them on the way here, and they are coming to offer you service.

HAMLET: Which actors are they?

ROSENCRANTZ: They are ones you used to enjoy—the tragedy-actors from the city.

HAMLET: Why are they traveling? They seemed to be doing well. Are they as well-liked as they were before, when I was in the city?

ROSENCRANTZ: No, indeed, they are not.

HAMLET: Why? Have they grown rusty?

ROSENCRANTZ: No, they are still good. But there is, sir, a group of child actors that now competes with them. The child actors are very popular now.

HAMLET: What, are they children? Who takes care of them? How are they fed? Will they quit acting when their voices change?

ROSENCRANTZ: There has been much argument about it, my lord. No one knows what will happen. But they are the reason the adult actors are on the road now.

(*Trumpets sound, announcing the* ACTORS.)

GUILDENSTERN: There are the actors.

HAMLET (*to* ROSENCRANTZ *and* GUILDENSTERN): Gentlemen, you are welcome to Elsinore. But I must tell you that my uncle-father and aunt-mother are deceived about me.

GUILDENSTERN: What do you mean, my dear lord?

HAMLET: I am mad only when the wind is blowing north-north-west. When the wind is from the south, I know a hawk from a handsaw.[5]

---

5. **handsaw** a saw used with one hand

(POLONIUS *enters.*)

POLONIUS: Greetings, gentlemen!

HAMLET (*aside to* ROSENCRANTZ *and* GUILDENSTERN): That great baby you see there is not yet out of his infant's clothes.

ROSENCRANTZ (*aside to* HAMLET): Maybe the old man is in his second childhood.

HAMLET (*aside*): I predict that he has come to tell me about the actors. Listen! (*aloud, to* POLONIUS) Greetings to you, sir.

POLONIUS: My lord, I have news. The actors are here.

HAMLET (*winking at his friends*): Really!

POLONIUS: Upon my honor.

(*The* ACTORS *enter.*)

HAMLET: Welcome, gentlemen! (*to* POLONIUS) My good lord, will you see that the actors have nice rooms? Make sure that they are comfortable.

POLONIUS: My lord, I will see to it. Come, sirs.

HAMLET: Follow him, friends. We'll hear a play tomorrow.

(ALL *but one of the* ACTORS *exit.* HAMLET *speaks to him.*)

Tell me, sir, do you know the play "The Murder of Gonzago"?

FIRST ACTOR: Yes, my lord.

HAMLET: We'll have it tomorrow night. You could, if I asked you, study a speech of some twelve or sixteen lines, which I'll write, and add it at a certain part of the play, couldn't you?

FIRST ACTOR: Yes, my lord.

HAMLET: Very well. Follow that lord,
And see that you do not mock him.

(FIRST ACTOR *exits.* HAMLET *speaks to* ROSENCRANTZ *and* GUILDENSTERN.)

My good friends, I'll leave you till night. You are welcome to Elsinore.

ROSENCRANTZ: Thank you, my lord.

(ROSENCRANTZ *and* GUILDENSTERN *exit.*)

HAMLET: Now I am alone.
Oh, what a rogue I am!
Am I a coward for not taking action?
I, the son of a dear father murdered,
Prompted to my revenge by heaven and hell,
Must unpack my heart with words.
Well, I've heard that guilty people sitting at a play
Have, while watching a scene, been struck
Deep in the soul by what they see on stage.
Sometimes a scene on stage will prompt
A guilty person to admit a terrible act.
And murder, though it has no tongue, will speak
During this play. I'll have these actors
Act out something like the murder of my father
In front of my uncle. I'll observe him carefully.
If he reacts, I'll know what to do.
The ghost that I have seen
May be a devil. And the devil has the power
To take on a pleasing shape. Yes, and perhaps
Because of my own weakness and my sadness,
He is taking advantage of me. I'd like to trust
The words of the ghost. But I cannot be sure
That it was really my father's ghost.

I need my own proof. The play's the thing
In which I'll catch the conscience of the King.

(HAMLET *exits.*)

Act 3

Scene 1

Inside the castle. KING CLAUDIUS, QUEEN GERTRUDE, POLONIUS, OPHELIA, ROSENCRANTZ, GUILDENSTERN, *and some* LORDS *enter.*

KING (*to* ROSENCRANTZ *and* GUILDENSTERN): Can you,
    By guiding the conversation, get him to tell you
    Why he has been acting so strangely,
    Destroying his days of quiet
    With such dangerous madness?

ROSENCRANTZ: He does confess that he feels distracted,
    But he will not speak about the cause.

GUILDENSTERN: Nor will he answer any questions.
    With a crafty madness, he keeps himself aloof
    When we ask him to tell us what is wrong.

QUEEN: Did he receive you well?

ROSENCRANTZ: Most like a gentleman.

GUILDENSTERN: But he seemed to be forcing himself
    To be polite.

QUEEN: Did you tempt him to any pastime?

ROSENCRANTZ: It so happened that we passed several
    Actors on our way here. We told him about it,
    And there did seem in him a kind of joy
    To hear of it. They are here at the castle now,
    And, I believe, they will be performing tonight.

POLONIUS: It is true. He asked me to invite
    Your Majesties to hear and see the play.

KING: I'll go with all my heart, and it makes me happy

To hear that he is interested in something.
Good gentlemen, tell him that we'll be there.

(ROSENCRANTZ *and* GUILDENSTERN *exit.*)

KING: Sweet Gertrude, leave us too,
    For we have secretly sent for Hamlet to come here,
    So that he may, as if by accident, meet Ophelia.
    Her father and I—lawful spies—will hide ourselves.
    That way, we may watch their meeting,
    And judge, from Hamlet's behavior,
    If he is suffering from love or not.

QUEEN: I shall obey you. As for you, Ophelia, I do wish
    That you are the happy cause of Hamlet's wildness.
    I hope that your goodness will bring him back
    To himself again, for the honor of both of you.

OPHELIA: Madam, I wish the same.

(QUEEN *exits.*)

POLONIUS: Ophelia, walk over here.

(*to the* KING) My lord, we will hide over there.

(*to* OPHELIA) Read from this book of prayers.
    That way, it won't seem strange that you are alone.

(KING *and* POLONIUS *exit.* HAMLET *enters.*)

HAMLET: To be, or not to be: that is the question:
    Is it nobler in the mind to suffer
    The dangers of outrageous fortune,
    Or to fight against a sea of troubles,
    And by fighting them, end them? To die is to sleep—
    Nothing more. By this sleep to say we end
    The heartache and the thousand natural shocks
    That flesh must suffer. It is an end

Devoutly[1] to be wished for. To die; to sleep;
To sleep, perhaps to dream. Ay, there's the rub.[2]
For in that sleep of death, what dreams may come,
When we have shuffled off this mortal coil?
Such thoughts must make us think twice
Before we do anything to endanger our lives.
We are willing to bear the whips and scorns of time,
We put up with the oppressor's wrong,
The proud man's insults, the pain of unhappy love.
Why do we bear such burdens,
Grunting and sweating under a weary life?
Because we are afraid of death,
That undiscovered country
From which no traveler returns.
This fear is what puzzles our will.
It makes us bear those ills we know,
Rather than fly to others that we know not of.
Thus conscience does make cowards of us all.
(*He sees* OPHELIA.) Oh, here is the fair Ophelia!
In your prayers, may all my sins be remembered.

OPHELIA: My lord, how have you been feeling lately?

HAMLET: I humbly thank you, well, well, well.

OPHELIA: My lord, I have some gifts of yours
    That I have been wanting to return to you.
    I pray you, now receive them.

HAMLET: No, not I. I never gave you anything.

OPHELIA: My dear lord, you know right well you did.
    And, with them, you said words so sweet
    That they made the gifts more rich.

---

1. **devoutly** sincerely
2. **rub** difficulty or doubt

Their perfume now lost, take them back again,
For to the noble mind, rich gifts become poor
When the givers prove unkind.

HAMLET: I did love you once.

OPHELIA: Indeed, my lord. You made me believe so.

HAMLET: You should not have. I loved you not.

OPHELIA: Then I was truly deceived.

HAMLET: Get thee to a nunnery! Why should you become
a mother to sinners? I am proud, revengeful,
ambitious. Why should such fellows as I be crawling
between earth and heaven? We are all scoundrels.
Believe none of us. Go to a nunnery.

OPHELIA (*shocked*): Help him, sweet heavens!

HAMLET: If you do marry, I'll give you this curse: Even if
you're as chaste as ice and as pure as snow, you shall
not escape gossip and scandal. Get thee to a nunnery,
farewell! Or, if you must marry, marry a fool. Wise
men know what you women do behind their backs!
To a nunnery, go, and quickly too, farewell!

OPHELIA: Heavenly powers, restore him!

HAMLET: I have heard about how you paint your faces.
God has given you one face, and you make yourselves
another. I'll say no more. It has made me mad. I say,
we will have no more marriages. Those who are
married already, all but one, shall live. The rest shall
stay as they are. To a nunnery, go.

(HAMLET *exits.*)

OPHELIA: Oh, what a noble mind is here overthrown!
And I am the most wretched of all women.
I heard the sweet music of his loving promises.

Now I see that noble and superior mind
Is like sweet bells that have been broken.
The music is now harsh, jangled, and out of tune.
Oh, woe is me,
To have seen what I have seen, to see what I see!

(KING *and* POLONIUS *enter.*)

KING: Love! His thoughts are not leaning
In that direction! There's something in his soul
That his sadness sits on, like a hen on her eggs.
When it hatches, I fear there will be danger.
To prevent that, I have decided this:
Hamlet must go to England. The king there
Owes me some money, and Hamlet can collect it.
Perhaps the seas and the change of scene
Will bring him back to his old self.
What do you think?

POLONIUS: It won't hurt to try. But I still think
That his grief is due to neglected love.
What do you think, Ophelia?
You need not tell us what Lord Hamlet said;
We heard it all. My lord, do as you please,
But I suggest that, after the play this evening,
You let his mother speak to him alone.
Perhaps she can find out why he is so unhappy.
Let him visit her in her room,
And I'll be hiding close enough to listen.
If he doesn't tell her anything,
Then send him to England, or confine him
Somewhere you think would be safe.

KING: It shall be so.
Madness in great ones must not unwatched go.

(ALL *exit.*)

Scene 2

A hall in the castle. HAMLET *and three of the* ACTORS *enter.*

HAMLET: Say the speech as I pronounced it
to you, trippingly on the tongue. If you bellow[3] it, as
many of our actors do, I would just as soon have
the town-crier speak my lines. And do not saw the
air too much with your hands, but use gentle
gestures. It is much better to act with a smoothness.
It offends me to the soul to see a wig-wearing actor
tear a scene to tatters. I would have such an actor
whipped for overdoing his part. I beg you, avoid it.

FIRST ACTOR: Of course, my lord.

HAMLET: Do not be too boring, either, but use your own
best judgment. Suit the action to the word, the word
to the action. Remember that the purpose of acting is
to hold a mirror up to nature. In other words, show
things as they are.

FIRST ACTOR: I think we can do that, sir.

HAMLET: Let those who play the parts of clowns speak no
more than is set down for them. Some actors will
laugh themselves, to get the audience to laugh, too.
That's terrible acting, and it shows a most pitiful
ambition in the fool that does it. Go, make
yourselves ready.

(ACTORS *exit.* POLONIUS, ROSENCRANTZ, *and* GUILDENSTERN
enter. HAMLET *speaks to* POLONIUS.)

My lord! Will the King be attending the play tonight?

POLONIUS: Yes, and the Queen will, too.

---

3. bellow   roar or cry out loudly

HAMLET: Tell the actors to hurry.

(POLONIUS *exits*. HAMLET *speaks to* ROSENCRANTZ *and* GUILDENSTERN.)

Will you two help to hurry them up?

ROSENCRANTZ *and* GUILDENSTERN: Yes, my lord.

(ROSENCRANTZ *and* GUILDENSTERN *exit*. HORATIO *enters*.)

HAMLET: Hello, Horatio! My friend, you are
The most sensible man I have ever known.

HORATIO: Oh, my dear lord—

HAMLET: I am not saying this to flatter you.
What advantage could I possibly hope to get
From a man who has no riches but his good spirits
To feed and clothe him?
Why should anyone flatter the poor?
Listen, ever since I could tell the difference
Between the qualities of different men,
I have chosen you as my friend.
Even though you have had some bad luck,
You have never complained.
You take the bad with the good, with equal thanks.
Blessed are those who can keep on going,
No matter what fate has in store.
Give me that man who is not passion's slave,
And I will wear him in the heart of my heart,
As I do you. But that's enough of this.
There is a play tonight before the King.
One scene of it is very close to the circumstance
That I have told you of my father's death.
Please, when you see that act being performed,
Observe my uncle. If his hidden guilt
Does not make itself known at that time,

HAMLET: It means mischief.

(*The* ANNOUNCER *enters.*)

OPHELIA: Will he tell us what this show meant?

HAMLET: Yes, or any show you'd like to show him. Do not be ashamed to show him anything. He'll not be ashamed to tell you what it means.

OPHELIA: You are bad, you are bad! I'll watch the play.

ANNOUNCER: For us, and for our little play,
We hope you'll like what it does say.
And now we'll start, without delay.

OPHELIA: That was brief, my lord.

HAMLET: As brief as a woman's love.

(ACTOR KING *and* ACTOR QUEEN *enter.*)

ACTOR KING: It has been thirty years
Since we met, fell in love, and got married.

ACTOR QUEEN: And may we be happy for thirty more!
But, woe is me, you are so sick lately.
I am worried about you.

ACTOR KING: Yes, I am sorry.
It looks as if I will be leaving you soon.
I am not as strong as I used to be.
My honored and beloved wife,
Perhaps you'll meet another—

ACTOR QUEEN: Oh, don't say such a thing!
There will never be another one for me.
If I marry again, let me be cursed,
For none wed the second
But those who killed the first.

HAMLET (*aside*): That's a bitter thought!

ACTOR QUEEN: The only reason to marry
  A second time is for money, not love.
  It would kill my first husband a second time
  The moment my second husband kissed me.

ACTOR KING: I'm sure you mean that now,
  But later, you might break that vow.
  Nothing is forever, so it is not strange
  That even our love might change.
  ,For here's a question we have yet to prove:
  Does love decide our fate, or fate decide our love?
  Now you think you will no second husband wed,
  But that might change when your first lord is dead.

ACTOR QUEEN: Dear, I swear that this is true:
  The only husband I'll ever have is you!

ACTOR KING: What a solemn vow!
  Sweet, please leave. I need to sleep now.

(ACTOR KING *falls asleep.*)

ACTOR QUEEN: Dear husband, may sleep refresh you.
  And may nothing ever come between us two.

(ACTOR QUEEN *exits.*)

HAMLET (*to* QUEEN): Mother, how do you like this play?

QUEEN: The lady does protest too much, I think.

HAMLET: Oh, but she'll keep her word.

KING: Have you already seen this play? Is there
  anything offensive in it?

HAMLET: No, no. They are just acting. The poison is not real.

King: What is the play called?

Hamlet: "The Mousetrap." It is based on the story of a
  real murder done in Vienna. Gonzago is the duke's

name. His wife's name is Baptista. You'll see. It is a play about evil, but what of that? Your Majesty and all of us who have clear consciences—the play has nothing to do with us. (FIRST ACTOR *enters.*) Watch this! This is a good part!

FIRST ACTOR: Evil thoughts, busy hands,
Strong poison, and no one watching!
It's perfect! This should do its work quickly.

(FIRST ACTOR *pours poison into the ear of* ACTOR KING.)

HAMLET: He poisons Gonzago in the garden for his money. The story is written in excellent Italian. You shall soon see how the murderer gets the love of Gonzago's wife.

(*The* KING *stands up.*)

OPHELIA: The King rises.

HAMLET: Why? Did something scare him?

QUEEN (*to* KING): What is wrong, my lord?

POLONIUS: Stop the play.

KING: Give me some light. Let's go!

POLONIUS: Lights, lights, lights!

(ALL *exit but* HAMLET *and* HORATIO.)

HAMLET: Why, let the stricken deer go weep,
And let the other deer play;
For some must watch, while some must sleep—
Thus runs the world away.
Oh, good Horatio, were you watching him?

HORATIO: Very well, my lord.

HAMLET: During the talk about the poisoning?

HORATIO: I watched him very carefully then.

HAMLET: Ah, ha! Come, players, let's hear some music!

(ROSENCRANTZ *and* GUILDENSTERN *enter.*)

GUILDENSTERN: My lord, may I have a word with you.

HAMLET: Sir, you may have a whole story.

GUILDENSTERN: The King, sir—

HAMLET: Yes, what about him?

GUILDENSTERN: He is very upset and disturbed.

HAMLET: From too much drink, sir?

GUILDENSTERN: No, my lord. He seems really ill.

HAMLET: Your wisdom should have taken you to the doctor with this news. If I go to see him, he would perhaps feel even more ill.

GUILDENSTERN: The Queen, your mother, in great affliction of spirit, has sent me to you.

HAMLET: You are welcome to visit me.

GUILDENSTERN: No, my good lord, you do not understand. Your mother asked me to tell you that your behavior has amazed and astonished her.

HAMLET: Oh, wonderful son, that he can so astonish a mother! But did she say anything else? Tell me.

ROSENCRANTZ: She desires to speak with you in her room before you go to bed.

HAMLET: I shall obey.

(*The players with recorders⁴ enter.*)

---

4. recorders wind instruments that have a tube, a whistle mouthpiece, and eight finger holes

Oh, the recorders! Let me see one.

Good Guildenstern, will you play upon this pipe?

GUILDENSTERN: My lord, I cannot.

HAMLET: I wish you would try.

GUILDENSTERN: I do not know how to play it, my lord.

HAMLET: It is as easy as lying. Cover and uncover these holes with your finger and thumb, give it breath with your mouth, and it will play most eloquent music. Look here, these are the stops.[5]

GUILDENSTERN: But I cannot get music from that instrument. I do not have the skill.

HAMLET: Why, listen to me! You would play upon me, you would seem to know my stops, you want to know my secrets. And yet, there is much music, excellent voice, in this little recorder, but you cannot make it speak. Do you think that I am easier to be played on than a pipe? Call me what instrument you will. Though you can fret[6] me, you cannot play upon me.

(POLONIUS enters.)

POLONIUS: My lord, the Queen would like to speak with you right away.

HAMLET: Do you see that cloud over there that's almost in the shape of a camel?

POLONIUS: Its shape is like a camel indeed.

HAMLET: I think it is like a weasel.

---

5. **stops**   holes on the recorder
6. **fret**   Hamlet is playing on two meanings of the word. One meaning is "to upset." Another meaning refers to the frets, or ridges, that guide the fingering on some instruments.

POLONIUS: Its back looks like a weasel.

HAMLET: Or like a whale?

POLONIUS: Very much like a whale.

HAMLET: Then I will come to my mother by and by. (*aside*) They'll say anything to please me. They think they are fooling me, but I know their game.

POLONIUS: I will tell her to expect you soon.

(POLONIUS *exits.*)

HAMLET: "By and by" is easily said. Leave me, friends.

(ALL *exit but* HAMLET.)

> It is now the very witching time of night,
> When all kinds of evil come into the world.
> Now I could drink hot blood,
> And do such bitter business as the day
> Would be frightened to look on. Now I go to my
>   mother.
> Oh, heart, do not lose your nature. Do not let
> The soul of Nero[7] enter my own heart.
> Let me be cruel to her, but not unnatural.
> I will speak daggers to her, but use none.
> After all, she is my mother. I am her son.

(HAMLET *exits.*)

Scene 3

A room in the castle. KING CLAUDIUS, ROSENCRANTZ, *and* GUILDENSTERN *enter.*

KING: I don't like the way he looks at me.

---

7. Nero a Roman emperor who had his own mother murdered

While he's mad, I don't feel safe.
And he's getting worse. Therefore,
Prepare yourselves to go to England with him.

GUILDENSTERN: We will get ready.
It is our duty to help keep you safe, your Majesty,
For so many people depend on you.

ROSENCRANTZ: Any person is bound
To defend his life with all his strength.
But a person whose life affects
The lives of many is even more important.
The death of a king is bad for everyone.
When a king falls, everyone in the kingdom suffers.
A king does not even sigh alone,
But with a general groan.

KING: Get ready, I ask you, for this speedy voyage.
We will put chains around this fear,
Which now goes about much too freely.

(ROSENCRANTZ *and* GUILDENSTERN *exit.* POLONIUS *enters.*)

POLONIUS: My lord, he's going to his mother's room.
I'll hide behind the wall tapestry
So I can hear what they say. I'm sure she will
Be able to find out what is bothering him.
I'll call upon you before you go to bed,
And tell you what I know.

KING: Thanks, my dear lord.

(POLONIUS *exits.*)

Oh, my crime is terrible! It smells to heaven!
Like Cain in the Bible story,
I have murdered my own brother.
I cannot even pray, though I wish to do so.

My stronger guilt defeats my strong desire,
And like a man with two things to do,
I stand here, wondering where I shall first begin,
And neglect both. What if this cursed hand
Were thicker than itself with brother's blood—
Is there not rain enough in the sweet heavens
To wash it white as snow?
If I could pray, what would I say?
"Forgive me for my terrible murder"?
I cannot be forgiven, since I still have
All those things for which I did the murder:
My crown, my ambition, and my queen.
May I be pardoned and still keep these things?
In this corrupt world, money can buy out justice,
And it often can buy out the law, too.
But it is not so in heaven. There is no trickery there.
What then? What remains? What happens
When one cannot repent? What a wretched state!
Help, angels! Do what you can.
Bow, stubborn knees. All may be well.

(*The* KING *kneels.* HAMLET *enters.*)

HAMLET: Now I could do it easily.
    (*He draws his sword.*) But no!
    If I do it now, he'll go to heaven.
    A villain kills my father, and for that,
    I, his only son, send this same villain to heaven.
    Oh, this would be a foolish act, not revenge.
    He took my father by surprise,
    With all his crimes on his head,
    As lusty as the month of May.
    And how his record stands now, only heaven knows!
    No, I'll not kill the villain now, when he is praying.

I shall wait. I will kill him later, when he is drunk,
Or angry, or doing some act
That would keep him out of heaven.
Then his heels may kick at heaven's door,
And his evil soul be sent below, where it belongs.

(HAMLET *exits.*)

KING (*rising*): My words fly up,
But my thoughts remain below.
Words without thoughts
Never to heaven go.

(KING *exits.*)

Scene 4

Queen Gertrude's room. The QUEEN *and* POLONIUS *enter.*

POLONIUS: He will be here soon.
Now, be firm with him. Let him know
That his behavior has not been right,
And that you have been trying
To keep him from harm. I'll hide here silently.

(POLONIUS *hides behind the wall tapestry.* HAMLET *enters.*)

HAMLET: Now, Mother, what's the matter?

QUEEN: Hamlet, you have offended your father.[8]

HAMLET: Mother, *you* have offended my father.[9]

QUEEN: Come, come, you answer with a foolish tongue.

HAMLET: Go, go, you question with a wicked tongue.

---

8. Gertrude is referring to King Claudius.
9. Hamlet is referring to his father, the late King Hamlet.

QUEEN: Have you forgotten who I am?

HAMLET: No, of course I haven't.
You are the Queen, your husband's brother's wife.
And—I wish it were not so—you are also my mother.

QUEEN: Do not speak to me that way!

HAMLET: Come, come, and sit down here. Don't move!
You will sit here until I set up a mirror
Where you may see the innermost part of yourself.

QUEEN: What will you do? Are you going to murder me?
Help!

POLONIUS (*from behind the tapestry*): Help!

HAMLET (*drawing his sword*): What's that—a rat?

(*He thrusts his sword through the tapestry, killing*
POLONIUS.)

POLONIUS: Oh, he has killed me!

QUEEN: Oh, my, what have you done?

HAMLET: I don't know. Is it the King?

QUEEN: Oh, what a rash and bloody deed is this!

HAMLET: A bloody deed—almost as bad, good mother,
As killing a king and marrying his brother.

QUEEN: Killing a king?

HAMLET: Yes, lady, that's what I said.

(*He lifts up the tapestry and discovers* POLONIUS.)

You wretched, rash, intruding fool, farewell!
I thought you were the King.
You found out that being too busy is dangerous.
(*to the* QUEEN) Stop wringing your hands.
Quiet! Sit down, and let me wring your heart.

For so I shall, unless it has become so hard
That it cannot be penetrated.

QUEEN: What have I done, that you dare
Wag your tongue in such rude noise against me?

HAMLET: An act that takes the rose
From the fair forehead of an innocent love
And sets a blister there. An act that makes
Marriage vows as false as gamblers' promises.
The whole earth is sick from thinking about the act.

QUEEN: What act? What are you talking about?

HAMLET: Think of the man who was your husband,
So good he was almost like a god.
Compare him to your present husband.
Are you blind? Can't you see the difference?
You cannot call it love, for at your age
The passion in the blood is tame, it's humble.
Who would step from my father to his brother?
What devil was it that fooled you into doing it?
Oh, shame! Where is your blush?

QUEEN: Oh, Hamlet, speak no more!
You have turned my eyes into my very soul,
And there I see such evil spots
That will never be clean.
Your words are like daggers in my ears.
No more, sweet Hamlet!

HAMLET: A murderer and a villain,
A wretch that isn't worth the small toe
Of your former husband! A monster
Who stole the precious crown and
Put it in his pocket!

QUEEN: No more!

HAMLET: A king of rags and patches—

(*The* GHOST *enters, in his nightgown.*)

>   Oh, save me! Protect me with your wings,
>   You heavenly angels!
>   (*to the* GHOST) What does your Majesty wish?

QUEEN (*not seeing the* GHOST): Alas, he's mad!

HAMLET: Have you come to scold your son
>   For not having taken revenge yet? Tell me.

GHOST: Do not forget!
>   You are not to hurt your mother. She is suffering.
>   Step between her and her struggling soul.
>   Speak to her, Hamlet.

HAMLET: Mother, how are you feeling?

QUEEN: Alas, how are you feeling,
>   That you look so carefully at nothing,
>   And have a conversation with the empty air?
>   Oh, gentle son, what do you see?

HAMLET: I see him, him! Look, see how pale he is!
>   Do you see nothing there?

QUEEN: Nothing at all, yet I see all that is there.

HAMLET: Do you hear nothing?

QUEEN: No, nothing but ourselves.

HAMLET: Why, look there! See how it steals away!
>   My father, in the same nightgown he used to wear!

(GHOST *exits.*)

QUEEN: You are imagining things!

HAMLET: Mother, I am not. For the love of grace,
>   Confess your sins to heaven.

QUEEN: Hamlet, you have broken my heart in two.

HAMLET: Oh, throw away the worse part of it,
And live more purely with the other half.
Good night, but do not go to my uncle's bed.
Pretend to be good, even if you are not.
Stay away from him tonight,
And the next time, it will be easier,
The next, easier still. For this,
(HAMLET *points to* POLONIUS) I do repent.
But heaven allowed it,
To punish me with this, and to punish this with me.
I will answer for the death I gave him. So again,
Good night. I must be cruel, only to be kind.
One more word, good lady.

QUEEN: What is it?

HAMLET: I must go to England. Did you know that?

QUEEN: Alas, I had forgotten.

HAMLET: There are sealed letters, and my two friends,
Whom I trust as I would trust two snakes,
Carry them. They will deliver the letters.
So be it. It's fun to see the hangman hanged
With his own noose. I know more than they think.
Now, I'll drag this body to the next room.
Mother, a final good night.
I'll see you in the morning light.

(HAMLET *exits, dragging* POLONIUS *offstage. The* QUEEN *exits after that.*)

Act 4

Scene 1

A room in the castle. KING CLAUDIUS, QUEEN GERTRUDE, ROSENCRANTZ, *and* GUILDENSTERN *enter.*

KING: There's meaning in your sighs.
    You must explain. We need to understand them.
    Where is your son?

QUEEN (*to* ROSENCRANTZ *and* GUILDENSTERN):
    Please leave us for a moment. (*They exit.*)
    (*to* KING) Oh, my lord, what I have seen tonight!

KING: What, Gertrude? How is Hamlet?

QUEEN: Mad as the sea and the wind during a storm.
    He heard a noise behind the tapestry,
    Whipped out his sword, cried, "A rat, a rat!"
    Then he killed the unseen good old man.

KING: Oh, heavy deed!
    It would have happened to me, if I had been there.
    Hamlet's liberty is dangerous to all.
    To you, to us, to everyone.
    Alas, how shall this bloody deed be explained?
    It will be blamed on us for not controlling
    This mad young man. But so great was our love
    We did not see what was best.
    Instead, like someone with a foul disease
    Who is trying to keep it secret, we let it feed
    On the very core of life. Where is Hamlet now?

QUEEN: He has taken the body away.

KING: Oh, Gertrude, we have to find him!
    Before the sun touches the mountains,

We will send him away by ship. This evil deed
Must somehow be explained.
Guildenstern! Come in!

(ROSENCRANTZ *and* GUILDENSTERN *enter.*)

(*to* ROSENCRANTZ *and* GUILDENSTERN) Friends,
We need your help.
In his madness, Hamlet has killed Polonius
And dragged the body from his mother's room.
Go find him, talk to him, and bring the body
Into the chapel. Hurry, please.

(ROSENCRANTZ *and* GUILDENSTERN *exit.*)

Come, Gertrude,
We must meet with our wisest friends,
To tell them what we plan to do
And what's already been done.
That way, perhaps we can avoid a scandal.
Oh, dear Gertrude, come away!
My soul is full of fear and dismay.

(KING *and* QUEEN *exit.*)

Scene 2

Another room in the castle. HAMLET *enters.*

HAMLET: There! Safely hidden!

ROSENCRANTZ (*from offstage*): Hamlet! Lord Hamlet!

HAMLET: What is that? Who's calling me?
Oh, here they come.

(ROSENCRANTZ *and* GUILDENSTERN *enter.*)

ROSENCRANTZ: My lord, where is the dead body?

HAMLET: I've mixed it with dust.

ROSENCRANTZ: Tell us where it is,
So we may take it to the chapel.

HAMLET: Do not believe it.

ROSENCRANTZ: Believe what?

HAMLET: That I can keep your secrets and not my own.
Besides, why should a sponge like you talk to the
son of a king like that?

ROSENCRANTZ: Do you take me for a sponge, my lord?

HAMLET: Yes, sir, one that soaks up the King's rewards,
favors, and influence. But people like you serve the
King best in the end. He keeps you, like an ape keeps
an apple, in the corner of his jaw. Soon you will be
swallowed. When he needs to know what you have
found out, he will just squeeze you, and, sponge, you
shall be dry again.

ROSENCRANTZ: I do not understand you, my lord.

HAMLET: I am glad of it. A clever speech means nothing
in a foolish ear.

ROSENCRANTZ: My lord, you must tell us where the body
is, and go with us to the King.

HAMLET: The body is with the King, but the King is not
with the body. The King is a thing—

GUILDENSTERN: A thing, my lord!

HAMLET: Of nothing. Bring me to him.

(ALL *exit.*)

Scene 3

Another room in the castle. KING CLAUDIUS *and several* ATTENDANTS *enter.*

KING: I have sent them to find Hamlet
    And to find the body. Hamlet is dangerous!
    Yet we must not lock him up.
    The people, lacking good judgment, love him.
    To keep them happy, his sudden leaving
    Must seem planned. (ROSENCRANTZ *enters.*)
    Rosencrantz! What happened?

ROSENCRANTZ: My lord, he will not tell us where
    The body is hidden.

KING: But where is Hamlet?

ROSENCRANTZ: In the hall, under guard,
    Waiting to be brought in.

KING: Bring him before us.

ROSENCRANTZ: Guards! Bring in the lord.

(HAMLET *enters with* GUARDS *and* GUILDENSTERN.)

KING: Now, Hamlet, where's Polonius?

HAMLET: At supper.

KING: At supper! Where?

HAMLET: Not where he eats, but where he is eaten.
    The worms are feasting on him now, just as they will
    feast on all of us.

KING: Alas, alas!

HAMLET: A man may fish with the worm that has eaten
    a king, and then eat the fish that has eaten that worm.

KING: What do you mean by this?

HAMLET: Nothing but to show you how a king may
   eventually travel through the guts of a beggar.

KING: Where is Polonius?

HAMLET: In heaven. Send a messenger to see. If your
   messenger does not find him there, seek him in the
   other place yourself. But if you do not find him
   within the month, you shall smell him as you go up
   the stairs into the lobby.

KING (*to some* ATTENDANTS): Go seek him there.

HAMLET: He will stay till you come.

(ATTENDANTS *exit.*)

KING: Hamlet, for your own safety,
   We must send you away with fiery quickness.
   Therefore, prepare yourself.
   The ship is ready, the wind is waiting,
   Your friends are packed. You sail for England.

HAMLET: England?

KING: Yes, Hamlet.

HAMLET: Good.

KING: Yes, it is good, if you knew our reasons.

HAMLET: To England, then! Farewell, dear mother.

KING: I am your loving father, Hamlet.

HAMLET: My mother: father and mother is man and wife.
   Man and wife is one flesh, and so, you are my
   mother.
   To England!

(HAMLET *exits.*)

KING (*to* ROSENCRANTZ *and* GUILDENSTERN):
   Follow him closely. Get him on board quickly.

68

Do not delay. He must be out of here tonight.
Away! Everything is ready. Go!

(ALL *exit but the* KING.)

King of England, if you value my good will
And fear my power, you will do as I say in my letter.
I want the immediate death of Hamlet. Do it,
   England,[1]
For he rages like a fever in my blood,
And you must cure me. Until I know it is done,
Whatever my fate, my joys were never begun.

(KING *exits.*)

Scene 4

A plain in Denmark. FORTINBRAS, *a* CAPTAIN, *and part of his* ARMY *enter.*

FORTINBRAS: Go, captain, greet the Danish king for me.
   Tell him that Fortinbras asks permission to march
   Across his kingdom. You know where I will be,
   If he wishes to speak to me face to face.

CAPTAIN: I will do it, my lord.

(FORTINBRAS *and* ARMY *exit.* HAMLET, ROSENCRANTZ,
GUILDENSTERN, *and* ATTENDANTS *enter.*)

HAMLET: Good sir, whose army is that,
   Who commands it, and why are they here?

CAPTAIN: Sir, it's the army of Norway,
   Commanded by Fortinbras. We are marching
   To Poland, to gain a little patch of ground

---

1. **England** He means "King of England."

That is not worth much.

HAMLET: Why, then, the Polish king will not defend it.

CAPTAIN: On the contrary, sir.
The Polish army is already there.

HAMLET: Thousands of men will die, and for what?
Thank you, sir.

CAPTAIN: God be with you, sir.

(CAPTAIN *exits.*)

ROSENCRANTZ: Shall we go on, my lord?

HAMLET: I'll be right with you. Go on ahead.

(ALL *exit but* HAMLET.)

How everything spurs me on to revenge!
What is a man, if his main activities are
Just to sleep and eat? A beast, nothing more.
Surely human beings are meant for more than this!
Is it forgetfulness, thinking too much, or cowardice
That keeps me from acting?
Look at Fortinbras—a delicate and tender prince,
He risks fortune, death, and danger
Even for an eggshell. Truly, to be great
Is not to act without good reason,
But to fight over a straw when honor is at stake.
What about me, then? I have a father killed,
And a mother dishonored, and I do nothing.
To my shame, I see twenty thousand men go to war
Over land that is not big enough for their graves!
Oh, from this time forth,
My thoughts will be bloody, or have no worth!

(HAMLET *exits.*)

Scene 5

ELSINORE. *A room in the castle.* QUEEN GERTRUDE,
HORATIO, *and a* GENTLEMAN *enter.*

QUEEN: What does Ophelia want?

GENTLEMAN: She speaks about her father. Her words
Do not make much sense.

HORATIO: It would be good to speak with her,
Before she says something that might be dangerous.

QUEEN: Let her in.

(GENTLEMAN *exits.* OPHELIA *enters.*)

How are you, Ophelia?

OPHELIA (*singing*): "He is dead and gone, lady,
He is dead and gone."

(KING CLAUDIUS *enters.*)

QUEEN: But Ophelia—

OPHELIA: Listen to this:

(*She sings.*) "At his head a grass-green turf,
And at his heels a stone."

KING: How are you, pretty lady?

OPHELIA (*singing*):

"Tomorrow is Saint Valentine's Day,
And in the morning time,
I'll be a maid at your window,
To be your Valentine.
So up he rose, put on his clothes,
And opened the bedroom door.
He let in the maid, for a while she stayed,
And left a maiden nevermore.

She said, 'Before you invited me in,
You promised we would wed.'
He said, 'It's true. I would have done it,
But you came too quickly to my bed.' "

KING: How long has she been like this?

OPHELIA: I hope all will be well. We must be patient.
But I cannot help my weeping, to think they should
lay him in the cold ground. My brother shall know of
it. I thank you. Good night, ladies, good night sweet
ladies, good night, good night.

(OPHELIA *exits.*)

KING (*to* HORATIO): Follow her closely.
Keep an eye on her.

(HORATIO *exits.*)

Oh, this is the poison of deep grief!
It springs from her father's death.
Oh, Gertrude, Gertrude,
When sorrows come, they come not one at a time,
But all at once. First, her father was killed,
Then your son left after his violent act.
The people are confused. They think that
I had something to do with good Polonius's death,
When all I did was foolishly, and in secret haste,
Arrange for his burial. And poor Ophelia,
Out of her mind with grief.
Now Laertes has come from France,
After hearing rumors about his father's death.
Oh, my dear Gertrude, I am worried!
(*He hears a noise offstage.*) What's that?
Where are my guards? Let them guard the door.
(*A* MESSENGER *enters.*) What is the matter?

MESSENGER: Save yourself, my lord!
   Young Laertes and his rebels are coming!
   The people call him "Lord," and then they say,
   "Laertes shall be King! We want Laertes!"

(*More noise.* LAERTES *and some* FOLLOWERS *enter.*)

KING: The doors are broken down!

LAERTES (*to his* FOLLOWERS): Sirs, stand outside and
   Guard the door. I need to talk to the king!

(FOLLOWERS *exit.*)

LAERTES: Oh, you evil king! Give me my father!

QUEEN: Calm down, good Laertes.

LAERTES: If one drop of my blood stays calm,
   It would betray my father.

KING: Why are you so angry, Laertes! Speak, man.

LAERTES: Where is my father?

KING: Dead.

QUEEN: But the King had nothing to do with it!

KING (*to* QUEEN): Let him go on.

LAERTES: How did he come to be dead?
   I'll not be lied to! Tell me the truth!
   No matter what, I'll have my revenge!

KING: Good Laertes, to get your revenge,
   Would you kill both friend and foe?

LAERTES: Only his enemies.

KING: Do you want to know who they are?

LAERTES: Of course!

KING: Why, now you speak like a gentleman.
   I am innocent of your father's death,

And am deeply in grief for it.
(OPHELIA *is heard singing.*) Let her come in.

(OPHELIA *enters.*)

LAERTES: Oh, heat, dry up my brains! May salty tears
Burn out my eyes! By heavens, your madness
Will be avenged! Oh, rose of May!
Dear maid, kind sister, sweet Ophelia!
Oh, heavens! Is it possible that a young maid's mind
Should be as fragile as an old man's life?

OPHELIA (*singing*): "They put him barefaced on the bier;[2]
Hey non nonny, nonny, hey nonny;[3]
And in his grave rained many a tear—"

LAERTES: If you had your wits and cried for revenge,
It could not be more touching than this.

OPHELIA (*singing*): "And will he not come again?
And will he not come again?
No, no, he is dead.
Go to your death-bed.
He never will come again.
May God have mercy on his soul!"

(OPHELIA *exits.*)

LAERTES: Do you see this, oh, God?

KING: Laertes, I share your grief.
Now, go and find your wisest friends.
They shall listen to both of us and judge.
If they find me guilty, I will give you my kingdom,
My crown, my life, and all that I call mine.

---

2. bier a stand on which a corpse or coffin is placed
3. Hey non nonny, nonny, hey nonny nonsense syllables

But if not, be patient.
I will find a way to make up for your loss.

LAERTES: Let this be so.
The way he died, his secret burial,
With no ceremonies or rites to mark his passing—
All these things cry out for explanation.

KING: And have it you shall.
Where the guilt lies, let the great axe fall.
Let us go now.

(ALL *exit.*)

Scene 6

Another room in the castle. HORATIO *and an* ATTENDANT *enter.*

HORATIO: Who wants to speak with me?

ATTENDANT: Sailors, sir. They say they have letters for you.

HORATIO: Let them come in. (ATTENDANT *exits.*)
I do not know who would be writing to me,
Except Lord Hamlet.

(SAILORS *enter.*)

FIRST SAILOR: God bless you, sir.

HORATIO: Let Him bless you, too.

FIRST SAILOR: He shall, sir, if it please Him. Here's a letter for you—if your name is Horatio, as I've been told it is.

(FIRST SAILOR *hands a letter to* HORATIO.)

HORATIO (*reading*): "Horatio, when you get this letter,

arrange for these fellows to see the King. They have
letters for him. Pirates boarded our ship on our
second day out at sea. In the battle that followed, I
boarded their ship. When our ship got away, I found
that I was their only prisoner. They have treated me
well, but they knew what they were doing, for they
expect a favor in return. Let the King have the
letters I have sent, and come to me as fast as you
would flee death. I have something surprising to tell
you. These good fellows will take you to where I am.
Rosencrantz and Guildenstern are on their way to
England. I have much to tell you about them.
Yours, Hamlet."
(*to* SAILORS) Come with me to the king.
Then you can take me to see my friend.

(ALL *exit.*)

Scene 7

Another room in the castle. KING CLAUDIUS *and* LAERTES
enter.

KING: Now you know the truth,
    And you must put me in your heart as a friend.
    Hamlet killed your father, and he tried to kill me.

LAERTES: It appears so. But tell me
    Why you did not punish him for these crimes.

KING: Oh, for two special reasons.
    First, his mother lives almost for his looks,
    And I love her too much to hurt her.
    Second, the common people love him so much
    That they see his faults as virtues.
    If I had sent any arrows his way,
    They would have returned to me

And not gone where I aimed them.

LAERTES: And so I have lost a noble father,
And my sister has been driven mad.
But my revenge will come.

KING: Do not lose sleep over it. You must not think
That I am going to forget what Hamlet did.
I loved your father, and I love myself.
Hamlet must pay for what he has done.
I am working on a plan.

(*A* MESSENGER *enters with letters.*)

What news?

MESSENGER: Letters, my lord, from Hamlet.
These are to your Majesty, and these to the Queen.

KING: From Hamlet! Who brought them?

MESSENGER: Sailors, my lord.

KING: Laertes, you shall hear them.
(*to* MESSENGER) Leave us. (MESSENGER *exits.*)
(*reading*) "Your Majesty, I am back in Denmark,
stripped of all my belongings. Tomorrow, I would like
to meet with you, ask your pardon, and tell you the
reasons for my sudden and strange return. Hamlet."
What does this mean? Did the others come back, too?
Or is this a trick?

LAERTES: I have no idea, my lord. But let him come.
It warms the sickness in my heart
To know I will have my revenge so soon.

KING: I have a plan to make your revenge look like
An accident. Even his mother will think so.

LAERTES: My lord, I would like to hear about it.

KING: Everyone says you are good with the sword.

Hamlet is jealous of your reputation.
He would welcome a chance to fence[4] with you
In a public match. He will soon hear of your return.
I'll arrange for people to praise your skill.
There will be a contest between you.
Bets will be made on both of you. He, being careless,
And not suspecting any foul play,
Will not examine the swords. You could easily
Choose a sword without a protective tip.[5]
In a practice pass, you can have your revenge.

LAERTES: I will do it. And to make sure he dies,
I'll put poison on the tip. I have some poison
That is so strong there is no antidote.
If I just scratch him with it, he will die.

KING: Let's think some more about this.
If this should fail, and anyone found out our plan,
It would be better if we had not even tried.
Therefore, we need a backup plan.
If you have trouble with the sword, try to tire him.
He'll call out for a drink. I'll have prepared
A goblet for him, which will be poisoned.
If he by chance escapes your poisoned sword,
We'll poison him with the goblet.

(*The* QUEEN *enters, in great distress.*)

QUEEN: One woe walks in on another woe's heel.
Your sister is drowned, Laertes.

LAERTES: Drowned! Oh, where?

QUEEN: There is a weeping willow near the brook.

---

4. **fence**   fight with swords for sport
5. **protective tip**   In the sport of fencing, the sword normally
   has a protective tip so no one will get hurt.

Near it, she was making flower chains. She decided
To hang them from the tree. When she climbed up,
The branch broke, and she and the flower chains
Fell into the weeping brook.
Her clothes spread wide,
And, mermaid-like, they held her up for a while.
She kept chanting parts of old songs,
As one who did not understand her own distress,
Or like a creature who lived in the water.
But before long, her clothes, heavy with water,
Pulled the poor wretch to muddy death.

LAERTES: Alas, then, she is drowned?

QUEEN: Drowned, drowned.

LAERTES: Too much water have you had, poor Ophelia,
And therefore, I forbid my tears to fall.
But I cannot help it. Let shame say what it will.
I have to cry. (*He weeps.*)
When these tears are gone, that will be the last
Of the woman in me. Good-bye, my lord.
I have a speech of fire that wants to blaze,
But this folly drowns it. (LAERTES *exits.*)

KING: Let's follow him, Gertrude.
How much I had to do to calm his rage!
Now I fear that it will start again.
Therefore, let's follow.

(KING *and* QUEEN *exit.*)

Act 5

Scene 1

A churchyard. A GRAVEDIGGER *and his* HELPER *enter, with shovels and pickaxes.*

GRAVEDIGGER: Is she to be given a Christian burial, even though she committed suicide?

HELPER: I heard that she is, so make her grave straight. The coroner has examined her, and he says it should be a Christian burial.

GRAVEDIGGER: How can that be, unless she drowned herself in self-defense?

HELPER: All I know is what they tell me.

GRAVEDIGGER: This is how I see it. Here lies the water; good. Here stands the man; good. If the man goes into the water and drowns, then he has done it to himself. But if the water comes to him and drowns him, he has not drowned himself.

HELPER: But is that how the law sees it?

GRAVEDIGGER: Yes, it is. It's the coroner's inquest[1] law.

HELPER: Well, do you want to hear what I think? If this had not been a gentlewoman, she would not be getting a Christian burial.

GRAVEDIGGER: Who knows, and who cares? Why don't you go down to the tavern and get us a drink?

*(*HELPER *exits.* GRAVEDIGGER *digs. As he digs, he sings.* HAMLET *and* HORATIO *enter.)*

---

1. **inquest** a legal investigation to determine the cause of death

HAMLET: Has this fellow no feeling for his business? He sings when he digs a grave.

HORATIO: He is so used to doing his job that he doesn't really think about it.

HAMLET: You're right. People who don't work much are the only ones who have time for delicate feelings.

GRAVEDIGGER (*singing*): "Age, with his stealing steps, Has got me in his clutch. And soon will put me into the ground, As if I had never been much."

(*He hits a skull with his shovel and tosses it up to the surface.*)

HAMLET: That skull had a tongue in it, and could sing once. How he throws it to the ground, as if it were nothing! (*He picks it up.*) This might be the head of a politician or a lord. And now he's just food for worms. His jaw is gone, and he's been tossed about with a shovel. Were these bones born for no other reason than to be used for playing games? My own bones ache to think about it.

GRAVEDIGGER (*singing*): "A pickaxe and a spade, a spade, Dig a deep hole for the latest guest. Get a burial sheet for the lovely maid She'll soon be here for her final rest."

(*He tosses a second skull up to the surface.*)

HAMLET: There's another. Could that be the skull of a lawyer? Where are his arguments now, his cases, and his tricks? Why does he allow this rude gravedigger to knock him about the head with a dirty shovel? Why does he not accuse him of battery? Or perhaps he was a great buyer of land. Is this what he gets for it—his fine head full of fine dirt? His deeds and papers would hardly fit into this box. Must the buyer himself have no more room than this?

HORATIO: Not an inch more, my lord.

HAMLET (*to the* GRAVEDIGGER): Whose grave is this, sir?

GRAVEDIGGER: Mine, sir. I am digging it.

HAMLET: What man are you digging it for?

GRAVEDIGGER: For no man, sir.

HAMLET: What woman, then?

GRAVEDIGGER: For no woman, either.

HAMLET: Who is to be buried in it?

GRAVEDIGGER: One that was a woman, sir. But, rest her soul, she's dead.

HAMLET: You are so careful with words. How long have you been a gravedigger?

GRAVEDIGGER: I started on the day that our last King Hamlet defeated Old Fortinbras.

HAMLET: How long ago was that?

GRAVEDIGGER: Don't you know? Any fool knows that. It was the very day that young Hamlet was born—he that is mad and has been sent to England.

HAMLET: Why was he sent to England?

GRAVEDIGGER: Why, because he was mad, and he shall recover his wits there. Or, if he does not, it won't matter there.

HAMLET: Why?

GRAVEDIGGER: No one will notice it there, for the men in England are all as mad as he.

HAMLET: Say, how long will a man lie buried in the earth before he rots?

GRAVEDIGGER: Oh, eight or nine years. A tanner[2] will last nine years.

HAMLET: Why does he last longer than the others?

GRAVEDIGGER: Why, sir, his hide is so tanned with his trade that it will keep out water a long time, and your water is a great decayer of your dead body. Here's a skull now. This skull has been here in the earth for twenty-three years. (*He picks up a skull.*) He was certainly a joker! He poured some wine over my head once.

HAMLET: Whose skull is that?

GRAVEDIGGER: This was Yorick's skull, the King's jester.

HAMLET: Let me see. (*He takes the skull.*) Alas, poor Yorick! I knew him, Horatio: a fellow of infinite fun. He carried me on his back a thousand times. I hate to think of this! Here hung those lips that I kissed often. Where are your jokes now, your dances, your songs, your flashes of merriment? Down-in-the-mouth, are you? Get you to my lady's room right now. Tell her that no matter how much she paints her face, she will end up like this. Make her laugh at that. Now, Horatio, tell me one thing. Do you think Alexander the Great looked like this in the earth?

HORATIO: Just the same.

HAMLET: And smelled like this? Yuck!

(*He puts down the skull.*)

---

2. tanner   a person who makes leather out of hides

HORATIO: Just the same, my lord.

HAMLET: Don't you find it interesting, Horatio, that the
noble dust of Alexander might end up as filling for a
knot-hole?

HORATIO: You think too much, Hamlet.

HAMLET: Not really. Alexander died, Alexander was
buried, Alexander returned to dust, the dust is earth,
of earth we make clay. Why shouldn't Alexander's
own clay be used to stop up a hole in a beer-barrel?
Or the great Julius Caesar, dead and turned to clay,
might stop up a hole to keep the wind away. But
that's enough. Look, here comes the King.

(KING CLAUDIUS, QUEEN GERTRUDE, LAERTES, LORDS, *and*
ATTENDANTS *enter.* BEARERS *carry a coffin.*)

> Who could be in the coffin?
> And why are there so few mourners?
> This suggests a suicide. It must have been
> Someone of high rank.
> Let's hide here awhile and watch.

(HAMLET *and* HORATIO *hide.*)

LAERTES: What other ceremonies will there be?

PRIEST: We have already done all we can
For her funeral ceremonies. Her death was doubtful.
Without the King's order, she would have been
Laid to rest in unblessed ground.
No more can be done.
We would dishonor the service of the dead
If we gave her the same rites
As we give to peace-departed souls.

LAERTES: Lay her in the earth, then,

And from her fair and pure flesh
May violets spring! I tell you, foolish priest,
My sister shall be an angel
When you lie howling.

HAMLET: What, the fair Ophelia!

QUEEN (*scattering flowers over the grave*):
Sweets to the sweet. Farewell!
I had hoped you would have been my Hamlet's wife.
I thought I would put flowers on your bridal bed,
Sweet maid—not on your grave.

Laertes: May countless woes fall on that cursed man
Who caused your madness! Don't bury her yet!
Wait until I have once more held her in my arms.
(*He leaps into the open grave.*)
Now pile the earth on both of us!

HAMLET (*coming forward*): Who is this
Who makes such a show of his grief?
This is I, Hamlet the Dane!

LAERTES: May the devil take your soul!

(HAMLET *leaps into the grave. They fight.*)

HAMLET: You do not pray well.
Take your fingers from my throat,
For, though I am not angry and foolish,
I have something dangerous in me,
Which, if you are wise, you will fear.
Take your hands away!

KING (*to* ATTENDANTS): Pull them apart!

QUEEN: Hamlet! Hamlet!

HORATIO: My good lord, stop this.

(ATTENDANTS *part them.*)

HAMLET: Why, I will fight with him about this
Until my eyelids no longer blink.
I loved Ophelia. Forty thousand brothers,
With all their love, could not love her as much.
What will you do for her?

KING: Oh, he is mad, Laertes.

HAMLET (*to* LAERTES): Did you come here to whine?
To outdo me by leaping into her grave?
Be buried alive with her, and so will I.
If you're going to rant and rave,
I'll rant as loudly as you.

QUEEN: This is madness.

HAMLET (*to* LAERTES): Listen, sir,
Why do you act like this with me?
I always loved you. But it doesn't matter.
Let Hercules himself do what he may,
The cat will mew and the dog will have his day.

(HAMLET *exits.*)

KING: Good Horatio, look after him. (HORATIO *exits.*)
(*to* LAERTES) Remember our discussion last night.
You'll soon have another chance to fight.
Good Gertrude, set some watch over your son.
This grave shall have a lasting monument.
Soon, a time of peace we'll see.
Till then, we must wait patiently.

(ALL *exit.*)

Scene 2

A hall in the castle. HAMLET *and* HORATIO *enter.*

HAMLET: I never finished telling you about

What happened on the ship.
We were on our way to England—
Rosencrantz, Guildenstern, and I.
In my heart there was a kind of fighting
That would not let me sleep. On an impulse—
Thank God for such impulses: this one might have
Saved my life—I got up and left my cabin.
Wrapped in my sailor's coat, in the dark,
I tried to find Rosencrantz and Guildenstern.
I finally found them asleep, and I stole their packet
Of letters and papers. Back in my own room,
My fears made me forget my manners and I opened
Their letter from our King to the King of England.
As soon as he finished reading the letter,
Without even stopping to sharpen the axe,
The King of England was to have my head cut off!

HORATIO: Is it possible?

HAMLET: Here's the letter. Read it at your leisure.
But do you want to hear what I did then?
I sat down immediately
And wrote another letter.
Do you want to know what I said?

HORATIO: Yes, my good lord.

HAMLET: I ordered the King of England,
In the name of our "friendship," to put the bearers
Of the letter to sudden death. They were not even
To have enough time to say their prayers. And
I signed it with the name of my mother's husband.
Luckily, I had my father's sealing ring[3] in my bag.

---

3. sealing ring Letters were sealed with melted wax, which
was then pressed with an identifying mark before the wax
hardened.

It matches the present King's seal.
I folded up the new letter, sealed it,
And put it where the other one had been.
Rosencrantz and Guildenstern never even knew
That the first letter had been missing.
The next day was our sea-fight with the pirates.
And you know the rest of the story.

HORATIO: So Rosencrantz and Guildenstern
Go to their deaths?

HAMLET: Why, man, they loved their work!
They are not on my conscience.
If they hadn't been trying to gain favor
With the King, they would still be alive.
When lesser men come between the swords
Of the mighty, they take their own risks.

HORATIO: What kind of king do we have?

HAMLET: Don't you think I already know?
He has killed my father and disgraced my mother.
He has popped in between me and the crown.
He has taken the position that was rightly mine.
Then he tried to have me killed!
Wouldn't it be perfect if I could put an end
To him and his evil?

HORATIO: He'll soon learn what happened,
When the King of England sends a message.

HAMLET: I'm sure he'll find out soon,
But meanwhile, the time is mine.
It doesn't take long to end a man's life.
But I am very sorry, good Horatio,
That I lost my temper with Laertes.
I'll try to make it up to him.

(*Young* OSRIC *enters.*)

OSRIC: Welcome back to Denmark, your lordship.

HAMLET: I humbly thank you, sir.
(*to* HORATIO) Do you know this water-fly?

HORATIO: No, my good lord.

OSRIC: My lord, I have a message from his Majesty. He
wishes me to tell you that he has placed a large bet
on your skill. As I'm sure you know, Laertes has
great skill with the sword. The King has bet six fine
horses that you are better. The exact bet was this: in
twelve passes between you and Laertes, he won't be
able to hit you more than three times. Laertes, on
the other hand, says that he will hit you nine times
out of twelve. The bet could be settled immediately, if
you would accept the challenge.

HAMLET: Sir, here is my answer: Let the swords be
brought. I am willing. If the King hasn't changed his
mind, I will win for him if I can. If not, I will gain
nothing but my shame and the odd hits.

(OSRIC *exits.*)

HORATIO: You will lose, my lord.

HAMLET: I do not think so. Since Laertes went to
France, I have been practicing. I shall win at those
odds. Even so, I have an uneasy feeling about this.
But it is no matter.

HORATIO: No, my good lord—

HAMLET: No, it's just foolishness. I try not to pay
attention to omens and bad feelings. There is a
special plan in the fall of a sparrow. If I die now,
I will not have to die in the future. If I am not going

to die now, I will still have to do it in the future. All
that matters is the readiness. Let it be.

(KING CLAUDIUS, QUEEN GERTRUDE, LAERTES, LORDS, *and*
ATTENDANTS *carrying swords enter. A table is set up with
goblets of wine on it.*)

KING: Come, Hamlet, come, and shake hands with
    Laertes. (HAMLET *does so.*)

HAMLET (*to* LAERTES): Give me your pardon, sir.
    Whatever I have done that may have offended you,
    I here proclaim was madness. I am sure
    You have heard that I haven't been myself lately.
    If I offended you, I certainly did not mean to.

LAERTES: I accept your apology.

HAMLET: Thank you.

KING: Give them the swords, young Osric.
    Hamlet, you know the wager?

HAMLET: Very well, my lord.
    You have bet on the weaker side.

KING: I do not think so. I have seen you both,
    And since he is better, we have odds.
    I think they are in your favor.

LAERTES (*finding that he has not been given the poison-
    tipped sword*): This one is too heavy! Let me see
    another.

HAMLET: This one's fine for me!

(*They prepare to duel.*)

KING: Here is some wine on this table.
    If Hamlet scores the first or second hit,
    I'll drink to his health!

(*They begin their swordplay.* HAMLET *scores the first point.*)

KING: Good! I'll drink to that! (*He drinks some wine.*)
Hamlet, this goblet is yours! Give him the cup.

(*He secretly puts the poison into the goblet and raises it as trumpets play.*)

HAMLET: I'll play this bout first.
Set it aside for a moment.

(HAMLET *and* LAERTES *continue their swordplay.*)

HAMLET: Another hit!

KING: I think Hamlet will win.

QUEEN: No, he's fat and out of breath.
Here, Hamlet, take my napkin and wipe your brow.
I'll drink to your good luck!

(*She picks up the poisoned goblet.*)

KING: Gertrude, do not drink!

QUEEN: I shall, my lord, if you don't mind.

(*She drinks and offers the goblet to* HAMLET.)

KING (*aside*): It is the poisoned cup. It is too late.

HAMLET: I dare not drink yet, madam. By and by.

QUEEN: Come, let me wipe your face.

LAERTES (*to the* KING): My lord, I'll hit him now.

KING: I don't think so.

LAERTES (*aside*): It almost goes against my conscience.

HAMLET: Come for the third bout, Laertes.
You are wasting time and toying with me. Come on!

LAERTES: All right! Come on!

(*They continue their swordplay. They fight fiercely, and* LAERTES *wounds* HAMLET *with the poisoned sword. Continuing to fight, they drop their weapons during a scuffle. Each one accidentally picks up the other's sword. Then* HAMLET *wounds* LAERTES *with the poisoned sword. At the same time, the* QUEEN *falls.*)

HORATIO: Laertes and Hamlet are both bleeding!

OSRIC: How did this happen, Laertes?

LAERTES: Why, as a bird caught in my own trap,
    I am justly killed by my own treachery.

HAMLET: How is the Queen?

KING: She faints from seeing you bleed.

QUEEN: No, no, the drink, the drink!
    Oh, my dear Hamlet—
    The drink, the drink! I am poisoned.

(*The* QUEEN *dies.*)

HAMLET: Oh, villainy! Stop everything!
    Lock the doors! Find the traitor!

LAERTES: It is here, Hamlet. Hamlet, you are killed.
    No medicine in the world can do you any good.
    In you there is not half an hour of life.
    The treacherous weapon is in your hand.
    The tip had no guard, and it was poisoned.
    The evil has turned itself on me. See, here I lie,
    Never to rise again. Your mother's poisoned.
    I can say no more. The King—the King's to blame!

HAMLET: The point is poisoned!
    Then, poison, do your work!
    (HAMLET *stabs* the KING.) And here,

You murderous Dane, finish this drink!
Follow my mother!

(*He forces the* KING *to drink, and the* KING *dies.*)

LAERTES: It is only fair. It was all his idea.
Let us forgive each other, Hamlet.
I forgive you for my death and my father's.
Forgive me for yours. (LAERTES *dies.*)

HAMLET: Heaven forgive you! I follow you.
(*to* HORATIO) I am dead, Horatio.
You live. You must tell the truth about what
happened.

HORATIO: I do not want to go on living.
There is still some wine in this goblet.

HAMLET: No, Horatio.
If you ever did hold me in your heart,
Keep yourself from happiness awhile,
And in this harsh world, draw your breath in pain
To tell my story.

(*An army is heard in the distance.*)

What war-like noise is this?

OSRIC: Young Fortinbras, returning from Poland in victory.

HAMLET: Oh, I die, Horatio. I won't live long enough
To see Fortinbras. But I predict that he will become
The next King of Denmark. He has my dying vote.
Tell him—(HAMLET *cannot finish the sentence.*)
The rest is silence.

(*The poison takes effect, and* HAMLET *dies.*)

HORATIO: There ends a noble life.
Good night, sweet prince,

And flights of angels sing you to your rest!

(*Sounds of marching are heard.* FORTINBRAS, *English* AMBASSADORS, ATTENDANTS, *and* SOLDIERS *enter.*)

FORTINBRAS: What's all this?

HORATIO: What would you like to see?
If it's sorrow or wonder, you can stop searching.

FIRST AMBASSADOR: This is a dismal sight.
Our news from England comes too late.
The person who gave the order cannot hear us.
Rosencrantz and Guildenstern are dead.
Now where will we get our thanks?

HORATIO (*pointing to the* KING): Not from his mouth,
Even if he were alive to thank you.
He never gave the order for their deaths.
I will now tell you what has happened here.

FORTINBRAS: Let us hear it right away.
Though I am sad to see this,
I have some rights to this kingdom,
Which I shall now claim.

HORATIO: I would like to speak about that, too.
But for now, let us honor these dead.

FORTINBRAS: Let four captains carry Hamlet,
Like a soldier, to his funeral.
Let soldier's music and the rites of war
Speak loudly for him.
Take up the bodies: such a sight as this
Belongs on a battlefield. Here, it is out of place.
Go, bid the soldiers to shoot.

(*A salute of guns is fired. Drums beat.* ALL *exit, following the bodies, which are carried.*)

SUMMARY OF PLAY

ACT 1

The Ghost of King Hamlet of Denmark appears to guards at Elsinore, the castle. Horatio, Hamlet's friend, also sees it. They agree to tell Hamlet about it.

Prince Hamlet's mother, Gertrude, and her new husband, King Claudius, talk to Hamlet. The King, who is Hamlet's uncle, tells him to stop mourning his father. Hamlet later talks to his friend Horatio. Horatio tells him about the Ghost. Hamlet agrees to watch for the Ghost that night. If it appears, he will speak to it.

Laertes advises his sister, Ophelia, not to take Hamlet's attentions too seriously. Polonius, their father, tells her to avoid Hamlet's company. She agrees.

That night, King Hamlet's Ghost appears to Prince Hamlet. The Ghost signals Hamlet to follow it. He does.

The Ghost tells Hamlet that he has been murdered by Claudius, his own brother. Prince Hamlet promises to take revenge against the King.

ACT 2

Polonius sends Reynaldo to Paris to spy on Laertes. Ophelia tells Polonius that Hamlet is acting very strangely. Polonius thinks he knows why. He thinks Hamlet is sick with love for Ophelia.

The King and Queen ask Rosencrantz and Guildenstern to spy on Hamlet. Polonius reports Hamlet's strange behavior to the King and Queen. The King and Polonius decide to eavesdrop on a meeting between Hamlet and Ophelia. They hope to find out if Hamlet loves Ophelia. A traveling group of actors arrives. They will put on a play at the castle. Hamlet asks them to include a few new lines that describe the death of his father. This, he thinks, will cause a reaction in the King, proving the King guilty of his brother's death.

ACT 3

Rosencrantz and Guildenstern tell the King and Queen that Hamlet seems fine. The King and Polonius hide, and listen to Ophelia and Hamlet. Hamlet tells Ophelia that he never loved her. The King is convinced that Hamlet is dangerous. He decides to send Hamlet to England.

Hamlet instructs the actors about his additions to the play. The play begins. The King is upset by the new scene, and leaves. Polonius calls for the play to end. The Queen sends for Hamlet to come to her room.

The King tells Rosencrantz and Guildenstern to go with Hamlet to England. Polonius tells Claudius that he will hide in the Queen's room and listen in during Hamlet's visit. Claudius tries to pray, but he cannot. As Claudius is kneeling, Hamlet enters with his sword. Hamlet considers killing Claudius, but decides not to kill him then. He will wait until a better time.

Polonius hides in the Queen's room while Hamlet visits. Hamlet, thinking it is the King, kills him.

ACT 4

The King decides to send Hamlet away at once.

Hamlet refuses to say where the body of Polonius is. He goes with Rosencrantz and Guildenstern to see the King.

Hamlet finally tells the King where the body is. Claudius writes to the King of England. He asks that Hamlet be put to death when he arrives there.

Fortinbras leads his army across Denmark on his way to attack Poland. They will fight over a worthless piece of ground. Hamlet decides that he, like Fortinbras, must act when honor is at stake.

Ophelia's strange behavior shows that she has lost her mind. Laertes and a mob break into the castle. The mob calls Laertes the next king. Laertes is very angry about his father's murder. Claudius finally calms Laertes down. He promises to help Laertes punish Hamlet for Polonius's death.

Horatio receives a letter from Hamlet.

Claudius receives a letter from Hamlet. It says that he is back in Denmark. The King and Laertes plan a duel, in which Laertes will use a poison-tipped sword against Hamlet. They also plan to have a poisoned drink for Hamlet, that will be used in case Laertes fails to stab him. Gertrude tells them that Ophelia has drowned.

ACT 5

Two gravediggers prepare the ground for Ophelia's burial. Hamlet talks about how death treats everyone equally. During the funeral, Hamlet and Laertes fight over who loved Ophelia more.

Hamlet tells Horatio about his experiences on the way to England. Hamlet and Laertes duel, and both receive fatal wounds. The Queen drinks the poison meant for Hamlet. Hamlet stabs Claudius, and also makes him drink the poison. Fortinbras returns from Poland. As Hamlet dies, he says Fortinbras should be king of Denmark. Fortinbras orders suitable funerals for the dead.

REVIEWING YOUR READING

ACT 1

FINDING THE MAIN IDEA

1. The most important thing in this act is that
   (A) Bernardo relieves Francisco of guard duty   (B) the Ghost tells Hamlet he was murdered by his own brother   (C) King Claudius sends Voltimand and Cornelius to Norway
   (D) Polonius gives Laertes some advice.

REMEMBERING DETAILS

2. The Ghost of Hamlet's father is wearing
   (A) a toga   (B) a nightgown   (C) a suit   (D) armor.

3. The Ghost wants Hamlet to
   (A) tell everyone the truth   (B) get revenge   (C) forget about his murder   (D) leave Denmark.

4. The Ghost has to leave at
   (A) noon   (B) 3:00   (C) once   (D) dawn.

DRAWING CONCLUSIONS

5. When the rooster crows, we can assume that
   (A) it is almost dawn   (B) he is hungry   (C) he is tired
   (D) he wants attention.

USING YOUR REASON

6. The real reason the King wants Hamlet to stay in Denmark rather than return to Wittenberg is that

   (A) he enjoys Hamlet's company   (B) he wants to be sure Hamlet won't rebel against him   (C) he doesn't think it is a good school   (D) he needs Hamlet's advice about how to run the country.

IDENTIFYING THE MOOD

7. Hamlet's mood in his first soliloquy in Scene 2 ("Oh, that this too, too solid flesh...") can best be described as

   (A) happy   (B) ungrateful   (C) troubled   (D) silly.

THINKING IT OVER

8. Do you think Hamlet's father was a good man during his life? Find evidence in the text to support your answer.

ACT 2

FINDING THE MAIN IDEA

1. The most important thing that happens in Scene 1 is that

   (A) Polonius sends Laertes a note   (B) Ophelia tells Polonius about Hamlet's strange behavior   (C) Reynaldo meets with Polonius   (D) Ophelia sews in her room.

REMEMBERING DETAILS

2. Polonius gives Reynaldo some _____ for Laertes.

   (A) clothes   (B) food   (C) books   (D) money and notes.

3. Laertes is studying in

   (A) Paris   (B) London   (C) Stockholm   (D) Rome.

4. Rosencrantz and Guildenstern are

   (A) soldiers   (B) officers   (C) friends of Hamlet   (D) from Norway.

DRAWING CONCLUSIONS

5. Hamlet says, "I am mad only when the wind is blowing north-north-west. When the wind is from the south, I know a hawk from a handsaw." From this, we can conclude that he

(A) is pretending to be mad   (B) is mad only on certain days
(C) knows a lot about tools   (D) knows a lot about birds.

USING YOUR REASON

6. The scene that Hamlet is planning to add to the play will probably remind King Claudius of

   (A) his wedding day   (B) his favorite holiday   (C) a play he saw once before   (D) the murder of his brother.

IDENTIFYING THE MOOD

7. Ophelia tells Polonius about Hamlet's strange behavior when he came to her room. Her mood at the time can best be described as one of

   (A) concern   (B) amusement   (C) boredom   (D) joy.

THINKING IT OVER

8. Do you think Hamlet is really mad? Use evidence in the text to support your answer.

ACT 3

FINDING THE MAIN IDEA

1. The most important thing in Scene 4 is that

   (A) Polonius hides behind the wall tapestry   (B) Hamlet kills Polonius   (C) the Ghost appears again   (D) Hamlet tells his mother he is going to England.

REMEMBERING DETAILS

2. Hamlet tells Ophelia that she should go to a
   (A) different city   (B) university   (C) nunnery   (D) park.

3. Claudius decides to send Hamlet to
   (A) Wittenberg   (B) England   (C) Russia   (D) Scotland.

4. Hamlet says that the purpose of acting is to
   (A) entertain   (B) tell a story   (C) show off   (D) hold a mirror up to nature.

DRAWING CONCLUSIONS

5. We can guess that Hamlet's directions to the actors in Scene 2
(A) are the same as Shakespeare himself would have given to
actors   (B) are foolish   (C) won't work   (D) will not be followed
by the actors.

USING YOUR REASON

6. One reason that Hamlet wants Horatio to watch Claudius during
the play is that
(A) Hamlet is not planning to be there himself   (B) Hamlet will
be too busy watching the play   (C) Hamlet wants to get Horatio's
opinion, to back up his own   (D) Hamlet wants to flirt with
Ophelia.

IDENTIFYING THE MOOD

7. Look back at the King's soliloquy in Scene 3, that begins with the
words, "Oh, my crime is terrible!" The overall mood can best be
described as one of
(A) satisfaction   (B) remorse   (C) innocence   (D) hope.

THINKING IT OVER

8. Why do you think Hamlet chooses Horatio, rather than a
nobleman, to be his friend? Find evidence in the text to support
your answer.

ACT 4

FINDING THE MAIN IDEA

1. The main idea in Scene 5 is that
(A) Ophelia is a good singer   (B) Ophelia misses her father
(C) Laertes wants to be King   (D) Ophelia loses her mind.

REMEMBERING DETAILS

2. In his letter to the King of England, King Claudius asks for
(A) the death of Hamlet   (B) a loan   (C) an invitation to a party
(D) information about the King of Norway.

3. In Scene 4, Fortinbras is going to
(A) a pyramid in Mexico   (B) visit friends in Denmark

(C) battle over land in Poland   (D) the coronation of the King of Norway.

4. Laertes is well-known for his skill

(A) as a dancer   (B) at chess   (C) as an acrobat   (D) with a sword.

DRAWING CONCLUSIONS

5. Look again at Hamlet's soliloquy in Scene 4. It begins with, "How everything spurs me on to revenge!" From this soliloquy, we can conclude that Hamlet

(A) admires Fortinbras   (B) thinks Fortinbras is a fool (C) thinks eggshells are worth something   (D) thinks human beings are beasts.

USING YOUR REASON

6. The reason Polonius has a secret burial, with "no ceremonies or rites to mark his passing," is that

(A) King Claudius doesn't want to draw attention to the death (B) Polonius doesn't deserve anything better   (C) this is what Polonius wanted   (D) this is all the country can afford.

IDENTIFYING THE MOOD

7. Read the last speech of Laertes in Scene 7. The overall mood of those words is one of

(A) confusion   (B) madness   (C) hope   (D) sorrow.

THINKING IT OVER

8. One of Hamlet's main problems is his inability to act in order to avenge his father. Why do you think he is having so much trouble with this? Find evidence in the text to support your answer. You can use evidence from previous acts, too, if you wish.

ACT 5

FINDING THE MAIN IDEA

1. The main thing that happens in Scene 1 is

(A) the gravedigger sings   (B) Ophelia's funeral

(C) the gravedigger tosses skulls out of the grave (D) Hamlet and Horatio hide.

REMEMBERING DETAILS

2. The gravedigger began his job on the day that
    (A) he turned 18 (B) Ophelia died (C) Hamlet was born
    (D) Yorick died.

3. When Yorick was alive, he was
    (A) a doctor (B) a lawyer (C) a politician (D) the King's jester.

4. The priest will not give Ophelia an elaborate funeral because
    (A) he thinks she committed suicide (B) he doesn't like her
    (C) nobody will pay for it (D) she died too young.

5. Queen Gertrude dies after
    (A) being wounded by a sword (B) falling into a brook
    (C) drinking poisoned wine (D) falling from a ladder.

DRAWING CONCLUSIONS

6. Hamlet believes that when Rosencrantz and Guildenstern arrive in England, the King of England will probably
    (A) let them go (B) have them killed (C) treat them as honored guests (D) check with King Claudius before doing anything.

USING YOUR REASON

7. Laertes is angry with Hamlet because
    (A) Hamlet never visited him in Paris (B) he is jealous of Hamlet (C) Hamlet has not avenged his father yet
    (D) he blames Hamlet for the deaths of Polonius and Ophelia.

THINKING IT OVER

8. Would you describe yourself as a "thinker" or a "doer"? Based on your answer, which character in the play do you think you resemble most closely? Explain your answer.